Detroit Free Press

THE LEGEND OF MR. HOCKEY

Gordie

<< *A masterpiece among men*

Gordie Howe will be remembered as one of the towering sports figures of the 20th Century. As the best hockey player of all time (Wayne Gretzky and Bobby Orr concur). As a reminder of a bygone time when even star athletes shared their lives with regular people. The day Howe died, Mitch Albom wrote: "Superman just bid us farewell. The comic book version had an 'S' across his chest. Ours had a winged wheel."
J. KYLE KEENER/DETROIT FREE PRESS

The lineup

EDITOR

Gene Myers

EXECUTIVE DESIGNER

Ryan Ford

PROJECT COORDINATOR

Eric Millikin

ASSISTANT DESIGNER

Jeff Tarsha

COPY EDITOR

Tim Marcinkoski

PHOTO EDITING

Ryan Ford

PHOTO IMAGING

Jeff Tarsha

DFP SPORTS DIRECTOR

Kevin Bull

SPECIAL THANKS

Bernie Czarniecki

Megan Holt

Beth Myers

Dora Robles Hernandez

Carlos Osorio

Mary Schroeder

Jacki Shipley

The Anchor Bar

No. 9 on the ice, No. 1 in our hearts

The hockey world mourned after Gordie Howe passed away on June 10, 2016. Two days later, for Game 6 of the Stanley Cup Finals between the Penguins and Sharks, T-shirts were placed in the stands in San Jose to display Howe's iconic number. In 1991, the expansion Sharks recruited Mr. Hockey for the debut of their teal jerseys with a shark biting a hockey stick. Howe and owner George Gund III skated in them for fans and media.
GARY A. VASQUEZ/USA TODAY

On the cover

FRONT: ASSOCIATED PRESS

BACK: MAIN PHOTO BY SALWAN GEORGES/DETROIT FREE PRESS; OTHERS FROM DFP FILES

Detroit Free Press

A GANNETT COMPANY

PUBLISHED BY TRIUMPH BOOKS   **ISBN:** 978-1-62937-392-8

TRIUMPH
B O O K S

TRIUMPHBOOKS.COM
@TriumphBooks

GORDIE
2   9

Gordie

THE LEGEND OF MR. HOCKEY

A night to never forget

The Red Wings' old guard — Gary Bergman, Ted Lindsay and Gordie Howe — donned their formal attire for the raising of the 1997 Stanley Cup banner. The trio and former radio voice Bruce Martyn reverently carried the banner down the red carpet.

KIRTHMON F. DOZIER/DETROIT FREE PRESS

Detroit Free Press

9 GORDIE **3**

His legend will live forever

Detroit's adopted son is gone, but the stories, on and off the ice, remain

MITCH ALBOM

Here's a Gordie Howe story. He was playing at the old Olympia, and an opposing player hit him and somehow cut his hand. Gordie had to leave the ice and go to the trainer's room. There, Dr. John (Jack) Finley, the Detroit Red Wings' longtime physician, began stitching him up carefully.

"Hurry up," Gordie said. "I gotta get back out there."

As Finley accelerated, Gordie added, "And by the way, Jack, don't go anywhere. Because the guy who did this is gonna be in here real soon."

Scotty Bowman, laughing, told that story to me a few hours after Gordie's death on June 10, 2016. Just as Wayne Gretzky told ESPN about being with Gordie at a White House dinner with President Ronald Reagan, and there were so many forks that Gretzky asked his childhood hero which one they should use.

"Kid, I have no idea," Gordie said.

"I'll follow the president and you follow me."

Who really follows Gordie Howe? Nobody can. Nobody will give us stories like that, or memories like those, not 25 years with a single team, not five decades of hockey, not a standing ovation at Joe Louis Arena as a white-haired, 51-year-old All-Star.

You lose athletes like this, and there's a hole on the shelf forever. Nobody slides over. Nobody fills the space.

A TV anchor asked me what other Detroit athlete's death was equal to Howe's? I had no answer at the time.

All I know is that Howe's death at 88 was seismic. Gordie Howe was the Babe Ruth of hockey. And you'd expect that Babe Ruth's death would be felt most strongly in New York, right?

The world should expect no less from Detroit. Howe's passing came on the same day as Muhammad Ali's funeral, and while the nation can lament two

CONTINUED ON PAGE 7

GORDIE 4 9

Spirit of Detroit

Besides his excellence on the ice and kindness off it, Gordie Howe was known for his sense of humor and storytelling skills. In a joint autobiography with wife Colleen titled "And … Howe!" he wrote: "Tiny Tim came to Detroit when he was really famous in the late 1960s, as I recall. I was surprised to find out that he was a big fan of mine. In fact, he signed a picture and they sent it over to the Olympia for me. It said: 'Dear Mr. Howe, Keep Puckering Those Nets.' The reporters asked me my response, and I just said, 'Well, it just shows that you can't always pick your fans.'"

SALWAN GEORGES/DETROIT FREE PRESS

Old-time hockey

Gordie Howe went with a fashionable hat instead of a tuque or helmet for the ceremonial puck drop at the Winter Classic Alumni Showdown at Detroit's Comerica Park on Dec. 31, 2013. From the left: Mickey Redmond, the Wings' first 50-goal scorer; Ted Lindsay, whose No. 7 the Wings retired in 1991; Mr. Hockey, who received a huge ovation; Brendan Shanahan, who won three Cups in Detroit; and Mark Howe, the Hall of Fame defenseman who received "a nasty look" — but no elbow — when he tried to assist his 85-year-old father.

JULIAN H. GONZALEZ/ DETROIT FREE PRESS

CONTINUED FROM PAGE 4

towering sports figures dying in the same week, there should be no criticism (as there was in some corners) for Detroit focusing its attention on Howe, even at the expense of Ali's funeral.

All sports are, at their core, local. It's why players wear the name of cities (or countries) on their jerseys, and why fans root based on their geography.

Gordie Howe was one of ours. He was "Detroit" and "Red Wings" with capital letters. His departure from this Earth was always going to be our biggest story of that day. No apologies. None needed.

People around the country asked what it was like in Detroit after the news spread. The answer: It was as if a top had been lifted from a boiling cauldron and an explosion of marvelous memories shot into the sky.

Bigger-than-life player

Who didn't know Gordie Howe in his city? Or his state? Who didn't have some kind of story or encounter? As with legendary Tigers broadcaster Ernie Harwell, it seemed everyone who ever shook Gordie Howe's hand was moved to remember it as a personal highlight. Someone will boast how he chatted with his youth hockey team and someone will tell you how he signed autographs in a parking lot and someone will detail how, if a child didn't say please or thank you, he would mark their palm with the pen.

Look left. Look right. There's someone talking about Gordie. The stories seemed to group into two categories:

The first sounded like panels in a Superman comic. As a child, young Gordie, born in a tiny Canadian farm town named Floral, grew strong carrying buckets of water into the farmhouse (his family had no indoor plumbing). Later he hauled bags of cement when he quit school to work in construction.

As a teen player he was 6-feet and ambidextrous, and could do things equally well from both sides. His phy-

CONTINUED ON PAGE 8

A man for all countries

Michigan's governor, Rick Snyder, and Canada's prime minister, Stephen Harper, revealed on the Canadian riverfront in May 2015 that the to-be-built $1-billion bridge between Detroit and Windsor would be called the Gordie Howe International Bridge. Howe did not attend the event, but his son Murray relayed his reaction: "That sounds pretty good to me." One playful Howe admirer tweeted: "Bad name for a bridge. Everybody knows that you don't cross Gordie Howe."
JOHN GALLAGHER/DETROIT FREE PRES

CONTINUED FROM PAGE 7

sique grew so chiseled, he could crush your hand when he shook it. He signed with the Red Wings, and his signing bonus was a team jacket. A team jacket? Yep.

"After I finished a game at the Olympia I used to walk home," he once told me. "Then, when I moved into a residential area, I took the bus down Grand River. You don't get too flamboyant on $6,000 a year."

Even so, he quickly fought his way into the league, and at 18 already was known as a brute force, at times, almost superhuman. During the 1950 Stanley Cup semifinals, Gordie suffered a serious injury crashing his head into the boards, and doctors had to drill a hole in his skull to relieve the pressure. Many thought he would never play again. Instead he came back the next year and led the league in scoring.

When does the Kryptonite come in? When does he grab Paul Bunyan's axe? That's what it's like to hear the first type of stories about Howe. He led the Wings to the NHL's best record seven years in a row. He won six MVP awards, won six scoring titles, held up four Stanley Cups and kept playing and playing, even as his once brown hair receded on that high, prominent forehead, until he looked more like a professor than a hockey player.

Well. From the neck up.

The rest of him was rugged hockey. Tough? He knocked out the famous Maurice (Rocket) Richard the first time they played each other. One punch. Nearly a decade later, when the New York Rangers' Lou Fontinato tried to ambush him, Howe hit him so hard "he demolished his nose," hockey historian Stan Fischler recalled. "I was there. Lou's nose took a 90-degree turn."

Fischler — who ranks Howe as "Top

CONTINUED ON PAGE 12

GORDIE HOWE
1928 - 2016

Bronze age

Gordie Howe checked out the resemblance when the Wings unveiled his statue inside Joe Louis Arena in April 2007. The statue — 6-feet-4 tall and 12 feet long — was composed of white bronze with integrated glass chips to simulate ice. The artist was Omri Amrany, who also created the statues of Tigers greats inside Comerica Park, Magic Johnson outside Michigan State's Breslin Center and Michael Jordan outside Chicago's United Center.

**ROMAIN BLANQUART/
DETROIT FREE PRESS**

A pair of Howes

That's Gordie and Mark Howe of the Whalers battling with a pair of Red Wings in brand-new Joe Louis Arena on Jan. 12, 1980. Mark had two assists and Gordie missed on three shots in a 6-4 Hartford victory. At one point, an octopus landed at Gordie's skates, which he scooped up with his stick and passed to a shovel-wielding employee. In the closing seconds, the organist played "For He's a Jolly Good Fellow." Howe then threw his gloves into the stands and gave his stick to Dennis Polonich, from Foam Lake, Saskatchewan, who had requested it.

**ALAN R. KAMUDA/
DETROIT FREE PRESS**

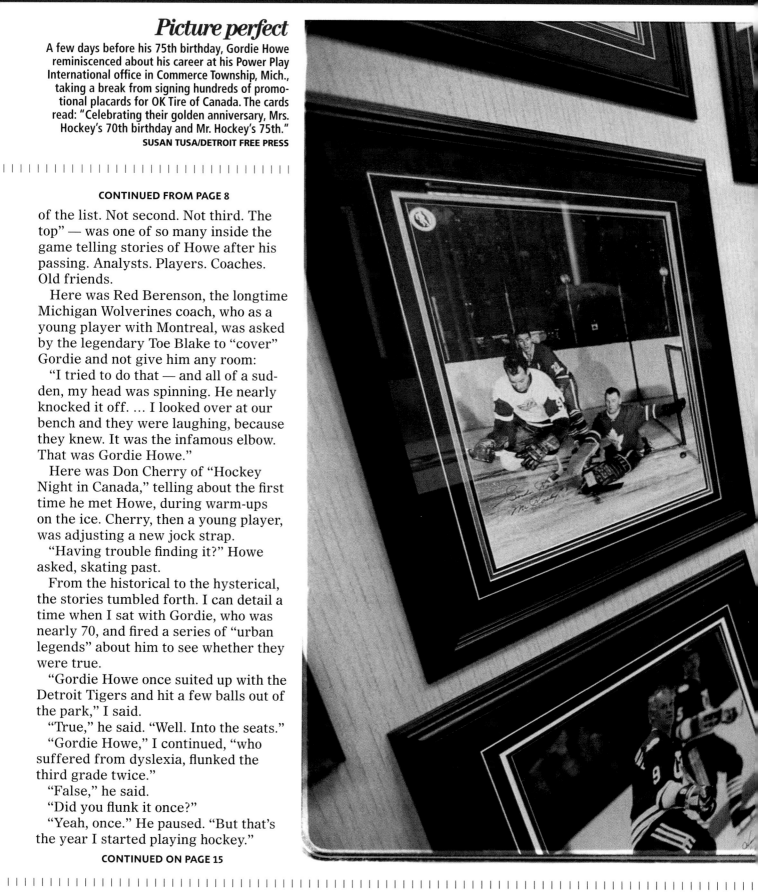

Picture perfect

A few days before his 75th birthday, Gordie Howe reminiscenced about his career at his Power Play International office in Commerce Township, Mich., taking a break from signing hundreds of promotional placards for OK Tire of Canada. The cards read: "Celebrating their golden anniversary, Mrs. Hockey's 70th birthday and Mr. Hockey's 75th."
SUSAN TUSA/DETROIT FREE PRESS

CONTINUED FROM PAGE 8

of the list. Not second. Not third. The top" — was one of so many inside the game telling stories of Howe after his passing. Analysts. Players. Coaches. Old friends.

Here was Red Berenson, the longtime Michigan Wolverines coach, who as a young player with Montreal, was asked by the legendary Toe Blake to "cover" Gordie and not give him any room:

"I tried to do that — and all of a sudden, my head was spinning. He nearly knocked it off. ... I looked over at our bench and they were laughing, because they knew. It was the infamous elbow. That was Gordie Howe."

Here was Don Cherry of "Hockey Night in Canada," telling about the first time he met Howe, during warm-ups on the ice. Cherry, then a young player, was adjusting a new jock strap.

"Having trouble finding it?" Howe asked, skating past.

From the historical to the hysterical, the stories tumbled forth. I can detail a time when I sat with Gordie, who was nearly 70, and fired a series of "urban legends" about him to see whether they were true.

"Gordie Howe once suited up with the Detroit Tigers and hit a few balls out of the park," I said.

"True," he said. "Well. Into the seats."

"Gordie Howe," I continued, "who suffered from dyslexia, flunked the third grade twice."

"False," he said.

"Did you flunk it once?"

"Yeah, once." He paused. "But that's the year I started playing hockey."

CONTINUED ON PAGE 15

GORDIE **9**
12

Sign of the times

Before Game 1 of the 2008 Stanley Cup Finals between the Wings and Penguins, Gordie Howe autographed a copy of "Nine" for Eric Prits, 11, of Oakville, Ontario. Several Howe autobiographies and biographies were published over the decades. The Wings' Bill Roose and the Windsor Star's Bob Duffy wrote "Nine."

AMY LEANG/DETROIT FREE PRESS

Long-distance well wishes

Five days after Gordie Howe's stroke in October 2014, the Wings-Kings game was delayed so that the Joe Louis Arena fans could stand and clap for Mr. Hockey. They also chanted "Gor-die! Gor-die!" So did the team on the bench. The next day, the Howe family posted a YouTube video of a smiling Gordie watching the tribute from his daughter's home in Lubbock, Texas.
RICK OSENTOSKI/USA TODAY

Signature talent

Among the Gordie legends was that he could sign his name 1,000 times in an hour. In "Gordie Howe's Son," Mark wrote about his father's nightly ritual during summer trips across Canada for Eaton's department store: "Dad would pre-sign 2,000 to 2,500 cards so he could spend more time the next day writing in things like 'To John, best wishes' and thus have more time with each person."
**ANDRE J. JACKSON/
DETROIT FREE PRESS**

CONTINUED FROM PAGE 12

"Gordie Howe, as a kid, would play with pucks made of 'frozen road apples,' another word for cow manure," I said.

"That's false," he answered, smiling. "I was a goaltender. And in the spring, that would be dangerous."

Humble champ off ice

Then there were private stories. The many moments of charity. The countless hours at a rink or a fundraiser.

The time Gordie photobombed a picture Kris Draper was taking with his son at Comerica Park, capturing a mock elbow throw beautifully. ("I'm so lucky to have that photo," Draper said.) Or the plane trip that Gordie took from New Orleans, sitting next to a woman whose husband, Roop Raj, was working as a Detroit TV newsman. The woman had no idea who Gordie was, and he never told her. Just spoke the whole trip about New Orleans. When they

landed, he gave her a card.

"Give this to your husband," he said. The card read "Mr. Hockey."

There are thousands of memories like that, being quietly told all over town, all over the state and, yes, all over the hockey-playing world. Make no mistake. It wasn't all storybook for Gordie. He served only four years as captain during his 25-year Red Wings tenure. "I did not like the captaincy," he once told me. "You're the one they come to and ask, 'What happened?'"

He also never made the kind of money that lets a legend retire for good (thus the many post-playing endeavors). And he wasn't thrilled with his retirement treatment by Wings management at the time.

"They didn't know what to do with Gordie Howe," he once said. "They had me in the front office. I think they were trying to embarrass me to leave. … Thank God the present ownership is

CONTINUED ON PAGE 16

CONTINUED FROM PAGE 15

different. ...

"I'd liked to have been an assistant coach, where I could play with the guys every day, and also be in a position where if two people got injured, I could go on the bench. If a third person got hurt, I could play five minutes."

It didn't happen. After all those years with the Wings and two years in retirement, he finished with a WHA stint playing with sons Mark and Marty and a final year in Hartford back in the NHL. Then came decades of just being "Mr. Hockey" — plus a one-shift appearance with the minor-league Detroit Vipers, which allowed him to say he played in six decades.

I joked with him before that game that he should be careful going over the boards. He said, "That's why I'm starting. I'll go through the gate."

His final years were challenging. Mrs. Hockey, his beloved wife Colleen, died in 2009 after a long struggle with Pick's disease, a rare form of dementia. Then dementia turned its sights on Mr. Hockey. A 2014 stroke that robbed him of his mobility and other functions had many fans bracing for the worst. (And reportedly had Gordie telling his family, "Just take me out back and shoot me.") But in true Howe fashion, he rallied once more, defying odds with unconventional medicine (a stem-cell treatment) and prairie stubbornness, putting the weight back on, regaining his strength, making a few more appearances to serve his legend.

The news of his death came suddenly to most of us. No long deterioration. No sad updates on failing health. He went quietly, with modesty, befitting a child of the Depression, who got his first pair of skates from a woman going door-to-door selling her possessions. Those first blades were too big, and he needed to stuff them with socks.

It was the last time any hockey shoe could not be filled by Gordie Howe.

He did it all. He left it all. "They used to say if you needed to fill a rink," Bowman recalled, "you'd probably go for Rocket (Richard). But if you needed to win championships, you'd have Gordie Howe on your team."

That's the kind of statement that makes a legacy. That, and maybe one more story from the second category, the kind that only gets told after an icon has passed.

In 1995, the Wings were in the Western Conference finals against Chicago, one victory from making the Stanley Cup Finals for the first time since 1966. Although they won the first three games, each by one goal and two in overtime, they had been embarrassed by the Blackhawks in Game 4 and some fans were worried about a letdown. Sergei Fedorov, a huge star, had an injured shoulder and was planning to sit out Game 5.

Gordie came to see Bowman. He told Bowman he thought it was essential that Fedorov played.

"Why don't you ask him to come down to the Joe tonight and I'll talk to him," Howe suggested.

Bowman did. Fedorov came down that night. They went out on the ice together. As Bowman recalled, "Gordie said to him, 'Sergei, you're not gonna get in to the semifinals every year. This isn't always going to happen. You got to suck it up and play.'"

Sure enough, the next night, Fedorov played. The game went to overtime again. It ended in double overtime, when Fedorov made an assist to Slava Kozlov, who buried the winning goal.

Twenty-nine years after the Wings had last been to the Cup finals, when

CONTINUED ON PAGE 17

Stevie, Gordie and Babs

When Mike Babcock met the press in 2015 to discuss leaving the Wings for Toronto, he brought along a paper from '05 announcing his hiring and a photograph of himself with Steve Yzerman and Gordie Howe.
ERIC SEALS/DETROIT FREE PRESS

Motown men

Two of the most famous names in Detroit sports history adorned Joe Louis Arena in November 2006 when the Red Wings named the 16-year-old building's main entranceway after Gordie Howe. He told reporters after the ribbon-cutting: "I said to Mr. Ilitch, 'Before I go out there, I just want to make sure that it isn't an exit.'" From the left: Ken Holland, Wings general manager; Mike and Marian Ilitch, Wings owners; Mr. Hockey, a Wing for 25 seasons; and Nicklas Lidstrom, Wings captain.
ERIC SEALS/DETROIT FREE PRESS

CONTINUED FROM PAGE 16

Gordie was a player, they were going again.

Howe was a bridge. A quiet, tell-nobody, era-to-era bridge.

You want to know what it was like in Detroit and in Michigan? That's what it was like. Story after story. Head shake after head shake. What Gordie Howe meant to his sport, what he meant to his fans, what he meant to his city and state, was still yet to be measured, because the memories kept exploding from that cauldron.

But I do have an answer for that TV anchor who asked what other Detroit athlete's passing compared to this one.

No one.

The world says farewell

Hockeytown turns out en masse to remember the greatest Red Wing

JEFF SEIDEL

Father J.J. Mech was filled with anxiety before officiating the funeral of Mr. Hockey, Gordie Howe.

"I was extremely nervous," Mech said, standing outside the Cathedral of the Most Blessed Sacrament in Detroit. "With such a legend, how do you encapsulate this?"

How do you capture the spirit of a legend? The essence of a hero? The legacy of the greatest hockey player ever in Hockeytown?

"It was an honor," Mech said.

Howe died June 10, 2016, at age 88. Four days later, from 9 a.m. to past 9 p.m., an estimated 15,000 people filed through Joe Louis Arena to view Howe's closed casket and visit with the extended Howe family. Then the following morning an estimated 850 people packed the church for a funeral that brought together everybody from hockey royalty to everyday fans — one man wore a Howe jersey, while a woman carried a giant "9" into the church.

The pews were filled with hockey legends from the past and superstars in the making.

From Guy Lafleur to Wayne Gretzky to 19-year-old Red Wing Dylan Larkin.

From coaches Scotty Bowman to Mike Babcock to Jeff Blashill.

From Michigan Gov. Rick Snyder to NHL commissioner Gary Bettman.

CONTINUED ON PAGE 20

A son on each wing

After a two-hour funeral, Gordie Howe's casket, with his son Marty at front left and son Mark at the front right, was carried out of the Cathedral of the Most Blessed Sacrament in Detroit on June 15, 2016. The other pallbearers included three grandsons and three grandsons-in-law.
ROMAIN BLANQUART/DETROIT FREE PRESS

GORDIE
18 9

Amazing grace

CONTINUED FROM PAGE 18

They all came to pay their respects, to honor this tough guy with the sharp elbows and the kind spirit.

This champion who helped bring four Stanley Cups to Detroit in the 1950s. This family man who raised his family in Detroit and Lathrup Village. This ambassador of the sport who never refused to give an autograph. This icon who was so big, so popular, that they had to shut down Woodward Avenue for his funeral.

"Gordie Howe was the reason this town is now called Hockeytown," Gretzky said. "I was lucky enough that I got to meet my idol, and then I was lucky enough to become friends with him. There are no surprises to me anymore about Gordie. Listen, I did book reports on him. I wasn't a great student. The only time I think I ever got an A on a book report was because I did a book report on Gordie Howe."

Ultimate ambassador

Before the service, a light drizzle started to fall, as Mike Mieduch stood outside the church at the front of the line, arriving nearly 4½ hours before the 11 a.m. start. "I'm here to pay respects to a person in the family," said Mieduch, 63, of Clinton, Mich.

Yes, Howe felt like family to everybody in Hockeytown, to anybody who ever met him.

But Howe was bigger than Detroit. He was an international icon.

Across Woodward, two Canadian national sports networks set up makeshift studios in an abandoned lot. Howe's funeral was broadcast live across Cana-

CONTINUED ON PAGE 23

Holy site

The Cathedral of the Most Blessed Sacrament, located at 9844 Woodward Avenue and featuring a Norman Gothic design, is the mother church of the Archdiocese of Detroit. Construction on the building started in 1913 and was finished two years later. However, the church's interior wasn't completed until 1930. Pope John Paul II visited the cathedral in 1987.

ROMAIN BLANQUART/ DETROIT FREE PRESS

Gift of giving

A glossy program at Gordie Howe's funeral included photos in uniform and with his family. It also included a series of quotes that reflected his work ethic and his humility. And a shout-out to a higher power. "I play religious hockey," Howe famously said. "It's better to give than to receive."
CARLOS OSORIO/ASSOCIATED PRESS

CONTINUED FROM PAGE 20

da, as well as across Michigan on Fox Sports Detroit and across the web on Freep.com.

"His reputation and what he did for the love of the sport, this guy is going to be remembered forever," Lafleur said. "He was one of the builders of the NHL."

Roddy Hogan was second in line and wore Howe's jersey. "Gordie was the best," said Hogan, 50, of Novi, Mich. "I'm here out of respect."

Two buses pulled up and dropped off several present and former Red Wings at the front of the church.

"I can't think of any athlete in any sport who represented our game as well as Gordie did," former Wing Chris Chelios said. "We were very fortunate to have him. I feel blessed that I got to be a part of the whole Red Wings tradi-tion and culture of the Red Wings."

A culture that Howe helped create, mass produced if you will, right out of the Production Line — the famous scoring line of Howe, Sid Abel and Ted Lindsay, and later Alex Delvecchio.

Not far away, Howard Haas sat in a wheelchair outside the church.

"What a wonderful man," said Haas, 90, of West Bloomfield, Mich. "He never turned down anybody to give an autograph. Ever!"

Haas was brought to the funeral by Tina Sawyer, a home health-care work-er, still wearing hospital scrubs. She remembered getting a Howe autograph at a restaurant. "The next time I met him, same thing," Sawyer said. "Kind, friendly, patient."

But who doesn't have a memory like that?

CONTINUED ON PAGE 24

Our father

Gordie Howe's children Cathy and Mark share a tearful good-bye to their famous father outside the Cathedral of the Most Blessed Sacrament. Howe's four children took turns caring for him in their homes during his later years until he settled in with Murray. He suffered his severe stroke at Cathy's home in Lubbock, Texas, in 2014 and died at Murray's home in Sylvania, Ohio, in 2016.
**ROMAIN BLANQUART/
DETROIT FREE PRESS**

CONTINUED FROM PAGE 23

Mr. Hockey was Mr. Autograph. Mr. Giving. Mr. Accessible.

In his words

Inside the church, a glossy program included several quotes from Howe that captured his essence, from his toughness to his humility to his selfless-ness.

Inside the cover, there was a Howe quote that summed up the way he lived: "You find that you have peace of mind when you know that it was 100% effort that you gave, win or lose."

There was a black-and-white photo of Howe with his family. He had four children, nine grandchildren and five great-grandchildren.

And there was a string of quotes that seemed to bring his voice alive:

"Good manners cost nothing."

"You've got to love what you're doing. If you love it, you can overcome any handicap or the soreness or all the aches and pains, and continue to play for a long, long time."

"I speak two languages: English and profanity."

"You don't need gloves, just stitch me up. And, in fact, don't go very far because the guy who did this will be coming in soon."

"I play religious hockey: It's better to give than to receive."

Amen to that.

So many stories

During the service, two police offi-

CONTINUED ON PAGE 25

CONTINUED FROM PAGE 24

cers patrolled the streets on horseback.

And Murray Howe, Gordie's youngest son, gave a rich, emotional, touching eulogy.

"He never accepted credit for any of his accomplishments," Murray said. "He credited God, his family, his friends, coaches, his teammates. And he never had a bad word to say about anyone, except for referees."

The tribute brought tears and laughter.

"He opened a door for a woman and she said, 'I didn't ask you to do that,'" Murray said. "And he said, 'Oh, I'm sorry, I thought you were a lady.'"

Everybody laughed.

"He shoveled his neighbor's driveway with about a foot of snow," Murray said, "and the neighbor came out and said, 'I didn't ask you to do that.'

"So he shoveled it right back onto the driveway."

Farewell to a hero

After the service, the casket was carried out of the church by Howe's sons Marty and Mark, three grandsons and three grandsons-in-law.

"It didn't matter who it was, when you came into contact with him, he made you feel like you knew him for years and years and years," former Wings tough guy Darren McCarty said. "And, like everybody said, he was the biggest practical joker there was."

Mark Howe, Gordie's middle son and a defenseman in the Hockey Hall

CONTINUED ON PAGE 28

Red is the new black

Mourners at Gordie Howe's funeral didn't just wear suits and dresses. The crowd estimated at 850 that packed the Cathedral of the Most Blessed Sacrament included people in No. 9 Red Wings jerseys and people carrying giant cutout 9's. Father J.J. Mech told everyone attending or watching the funeral: "We're family because we have been affected."

ROMAIN BLANQUART/ DETROIT FREE PRESS

9 GORDIE **25**

For more than 12 hours — 9 a.m. to past 9 p.m. — an estimated 15,000 fans came to Joe Louis Arena to pay their respects to Mr. Hockey. His extended family took shifts greeting mourners. Columnist Drew Sharp described it this way in the Free Press: "The old. The young. The known. The anonymous. They lined up outside around the southwest corner of Joe Louis Arena, sometimes more than 300 deep in the early afternoon. The woolen, long-sleeved No. 9 winged wheel sweaters that many wore not exactly meshing well with the springtime heat. But those paying tribute to Gordie Howe patiently waited for as long as two hours without complaint."

"Gordie Howe was the reason this town is now called Hockeytown."

WAYNE GRETZKY, on Gordie's legacy in Detroit and in the world of hockey

Terrible & Great

Hockey legends Ted (Terrible Ted) Lindsay and Wayne (The Great One) Gretzky acknowledged their good friend Gordie (Mr. Hockey) Howe before his funeral at the Cathedral of the Most Blessed Sacrament. Lindsay said: "Gordie really was the greatest hockey player who ever lived." Gretzky concurred.

CARLOS OSORIO/ASSOCIATED PRESS

CONTINUED FROM PAGE 25

of Fame, was overcome with emotion, standing outside the church.

"It's a tough time," he said. "We know what an absolute treasure of a human being my father was. We are trying to celebrate his life. It's hard for me right now.

"I said in my Hall of Fame speech, he is a role model of everything I try to be as a human being. I had to admit, unfortunately, I can't keep up to his standards but I try.

"I'm hoping and praying that him and Mom are having a wonderful time together right now."

Then, several Red Wings got onto two buses. Each bus had an electronic sign on the front that blinked: "Gordie Howe Mr. Hockey Farewell."

Farewell indeed.

A tribute with humor & humility

HELENE ST. JAMES

The eulogy celebrated Gordie Howe for his legendary career, his equally legendary humility and his radiant joy.

Howe's funeral lasted two hours and was attended by dozens of hockey dignitaries, reflecting how many lives the Detroit Red Wings legend touched. One of the most touching moments came near the end of youngest son Murray Howe's nearly half-hour tribute to the man known as Mr. Hockey.

"I asked my dad a few years ago what he would like me to say at his funeral," Murray said June 15, 2016, at the Cathedral of the Most Blessed Sacrament in Detroit. "He said, 'Say this: Finally, the end of the third period.' Then he added, 'I hope there is a good hockey team in heaven.'

"Dad, all I can say is, once you join the team, they won't just be good, they will be great."

Gordie Howe had died five days earlier at age 88.

"How do I do justice to the life of a living legend, my own hero?" Murray began in front of a crowd that included Steve Yzerman, Wayne Gretzky, Scotty Bowman, Chris Chelios, Guy Lafleur, Mike Babcock and Gary Bettman, among many others. "I still pinch myself at the realization that he was my father."

Murray used anecdote after anecdote

CONTINUED ON PAGE 30

CONTINUED FROM PAGE 29

to demonstrate how Gordie Howe lived an outsized life.

"There are endless superlatives that come to mind when describing my dad," Murray said. "Humble. A man came over for an autograph, and a woman saw him signing something, and she rushed over and said, 'Are you somebody famous?' And he said, 'No, I just used to babysit that guy.'

"He was tough. Even when it was negative-50 in Saskatoon, he would say there's no such thing as cold weather, only cold clothing. I was helping him do a hardware project up at our cabin, and he smashed his thumb with a two-pound hammer, and blood was just squirting everywhere. He shakes his thumb a little bit and then he just keeps on going. It was broken.

"Dad was wise. He was a man of few words, but everything he said was worth hearing. Such as, 'A good bodycheck will be remembered.' Wayne Gretzky at the age of 10 was at an awards banquet with my dad, and the emcee mistakenly asked Wayne to say a few words to accept his award, forgetting that Wayne was only 10 years old. Mr. Hockey grabbed the microphone and said, 'Anyone who scores 378 goals in a season doesn't need to say another word.'

"Mr. Hockey was graceful. He always looked so effortless, whether he was skating, swinging a golf club, chopping wood or wielding his favorite tool, a sledgehammer. Even in his last years, as his balance waned, the few times that he fell, he rolled gracefully and popped back up with a grin.

"He was powerful. Who else do you know could crack open lobster claws with their fingers? Or bring any man to his knees with a handshake?

"He was prompt. He was never late for anything. To him, it was courtesy. He made it a point to show up early and chat with whomever he happened to meet. It was not surprising to find him helping the servers to set up tables at events where he was the featured

speaker."

There were funny stories of what it was like to grow up with a man legendary for his backbone. Gordie and Colleen Howe, who died in 2009, had four children: sons Murray, Marty and Mark and daughter Cathy.

"I never heard him complain about anything, ever," Murray said. "The downside to that was, as kids, we were never allowed to complain about anything. So if we lamented about raking

CONTINUED ON PAGE 31

And ... Howe!

Tom Fowlow, 73, of Bloomfield Hills, Mich., checked out the messages of love, support and Godspeed that would fill two giant "Thank you, Mr. Hockey" boards hanging on Joe Louis Arena outside a street-level entrance. In one scene, a little boy, holding his father's hand, pointed to all the messages and said: "He knew a lot of people."
ERIC SEALS/DETROIT FREE PRESS

HOCKEY

GORDIE HOWE
1928-2016

Portrait of a winner

After hearing the news that Gordie Howe had passed, Cole Brazle of Clawson, Mich., spent 10 hours working on an oil on canvas painting of Mr. Hockey. Brazle, 22, brought it to the Joe Louis Arena visitation to give to the Howe family. Before long, it was on the stage near Howe's casket.
ERIC SEALS/DETROIT FREE PRESS

"I hope there is a good hockey team in heaven."

GORDIE HOWE, to his son Murray during their discussion about his eulogy

CONTINUED FROM PAGE 30

for four hours straight outside, he'd just bring out his miniature, invisible violin and go, 'So sorry for you.' Stopped us whining in our tracks.

"He was eternally positive. He always had a smile on his face and a song on his lips."

The eulogy hit just the right balance of reverence with a dash of irreverence.

"He was patient," Murry said. "No matter how bad the circumstances, never once did I hear him raise his voice. He didn't need to. If a fan told him a story, he would not interrupt, no matter how long they spoke. And he would not correct them, even if they insisted they watched him play in the Summer Olympics in 1906.

"He accepted everyone for who they were, unless they were a boy with long hair. Then they got a lecture."

There was a loving moment remembered from childhood, back when Mark would race Marty home from school. One time, Mark arrived to find Marty already seated in the kitchen. It turned out he had been sent home early because a classmate had dissed Gordie, and Marty "turned around and cleaned

CONTINUED ON PAGE 32

CONTINUED FROM PAGE 31

his clock," Murray said. Colleen read the riot act to Marty, then to Gordie when he arrived home. When she left the room, Gordie walked up to Marty, smiled and whispered, "Good job."

Murray shared several stories from the past few years of Howe's life. He lived part of the time with his daughter in Lubbock, Texas, and part of it with Murray in Sylvania, Ohio. The two were out for a walk near a university one day, when Gordie commented that "this is the closest I've ever been to college," Murray said. Then there was the time Gordie was talking to a woman who worked for the FBI, and he told her he knew where Jimmy Hoffa was buried. Leaning in to make sure no one could overhear, Murray said, "He told her, 'In the ground.'"

As he neared the end of the eulogy, the tone became touching.

"A stroke hit my dad so hard at 86 that I wrote his eulogy at that time," said Murray, a doctor specializing in radiology. "But the comeback came with an assist from some stem cells, and he decided to hang on for an unforgettable year-and-a-half victory lap."

For several weeks, family members noticed Gordie was declining again.

"It was clear that he was no longer having fun," Murray said. "Dad always said, 'If it's not fun, it's time to do something else.' So we filled his final days, surrounding him with friends and family, and he knew he was loved. Mr. Hockey left the world with no regrets. And although he did not lead the league in church attendance, his life has been the epitome of a faithful servant."

Murray said farewell with two final blessings:

"Shalom. I wish for you the good Lord's eternal peace, comfort and joy, just as you gave us while you were in our midst.

"Namaste. I humbly bow to you. Dad, for your magnificent example for all of us, we will do our best to follow your lead until we meet again. Thank you."

End of the line

The lunchtime line stretched around a good part of the Joe for fans who wanted to say their farewells to Gordie Howe. The first person in line was Bud Somerville, a Detroit native who arrived at 11:30 the previous night. He said he wasn't trying to make a statement, just to show respect, "to see Gordie, thank him and thank the family." He also said he had met Mr. Hockey "hundreds of times" at autograph shows, restaurants, Olympia Stadium and the Joe. The next person in line came at 6:45 a.m., still 2¼ hours before the visitation.
ERIC SEALS/DETROIT FREE PRESS

He made everyone feel welcome

SHAWN WINDSOR

Vernon Harris grew up loving hockey even though hockey didn't love him. That's how it felt to Harris, anyway, who once tried to play for a youth team at Olympia Stadium in Detroit but was told "Negroes weren't allowed."

"I accepted that," he said.

Gordie Howe didn't. He welcomed Harris when he spotted him at Olympia waiting near the locker rooms after Red Wings games.

"I always called him Mr. Howe, and he always stopped to give me his autograph and say hello," Harris said.

That fundamental interaction helped give Harris the courage to keep coming to games at Olympia and turned Harris into a lifelong Wings fan. It also brought him to Joe Louis Arena to pay respects to the man who made him feel welcome all those years ago.

Harris, 70, waited in line for maybe an hour to offer condolences to the Howe family and lay a hand on Mr. Howe's casket. He told Mark Howe, Gordie's middle son, that his dad always had been friendly to him.

Beyond that, Harris appreciated the old man's puck-handling ability and toughness.

"Guys would crowd him, and he'd use those elbows to knock them off," Harris said. "He wasn't a dirty player. He just defended himself. He played the

CONTINUED ON PAGE 34

A lifelong fan

Vernon Harris of Westland, Mich., grew up in Detroit not far from Olympia Stadium, where he would go see Gordie Howe's Red Wings but wasn't allowed to play youth hockey because of racial discrimination in the city.
HARRIS FAMILY

CONTINUED FROM PAGE 33

game for respect. That's what I liked."

Harris, who now resides in Westland, Mich., grew up six blocks from Olympia and played street hockey using a tennis ball and a couple of banged-up sticks. He and his friends turned the space between cars on the curb into their nets. He tried to convince his buddies to attend games with him — back then, Saturday afternoon matinees were as cheap as $2 — but they weren't comfortable around the sport.

"They were scared," Harris said. "There was one (black) player in the NHL then, Willie O'Ree, who played for the Boston Bruins."

Harris left Detroit in the middle 1960s to join the Navy. After three tours of duty in Vietnam, he returned home and worked for the city's water department for three decades.

All along, he kept attending Wings games and even hit other NHL arenas from time to time. In 60 years as a hockey fan, he never loved a player more than Howe.

He is the reason Harris learned to skate. The reason he follows hockey. The reason he took time to trek downtown, to nod to a man who helped him in ways he never knew.

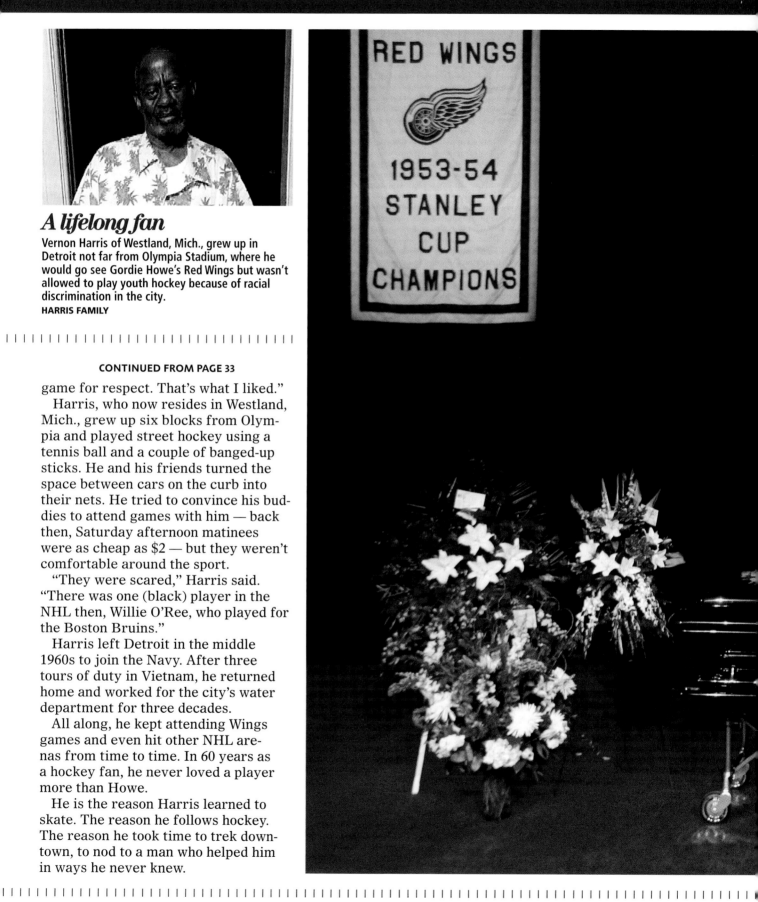

Every fan has a story

Why did so many people — an estimated 15,000 — wait in line — sometimes for two hours — for one final encounter with Gordie Howe? Jay Crawford, 92, of Ferndale, Mich., attended the visitation with his 67-year-old son, Terry, and provided an excellent explanation. "He was a humble man," he said. "A regular guy. Fans here could relate to that." The older Crawford said he saw Howe's first NHL game in 1946 (at Olympia at age 18) and his last NHL game in 1980 (with the Whalers at age 52).

CARLOS OSORIO/ ASSOCIATED PRESS

A player unlike any other

A star who shined brightest after he faded into the background

BILL MCGRAW & HELENE ST. JAMES

He played one of the world's most demanding games until he was 52 years old, and many fans argue that no one played it better.

His pro career of 2,421 games ran from World War II through Vietnam, Truman to Carter, Sinatra to the Sex Pistols.

He lasted so long that he played professionally with his children.

Gordie Howe, who died June 10, 2016, at age 88, combined skill, savvy, strength, meanness and longevity like no other hockey player. He was among the greatest sports stars of the 20th Century, and he reigned in the trinity of Detroit's paramount athletes, with Joe Louis and Ty Cobb.

Howe died in Sylvania, Ohio. He had been staying there with his son Murray. Howe had suffered from dementia in his later years and suffered a stroke in October 2014. Stem-cell treatment helped him rally from near-death,

and celebrations for his last birthday, March 31, included a visit to Joe Louis Arena.

Howe spent 25 years as a Red Wing and lived in southeast Michigan for most of his long retirement. He was an extraordinarily public person who encountered thousands of people over the years. He remained a megastar who happened to be unassuming, playful and patient, and he often had a kind word or gentle gibe for every fan.

Howe had a dry wit, and he frequently used it to disarm awestruck audiences. Speaking to French Canadians, he would say, "I'm bilingual: English and profanity."

Many of his public appearances were organized by his late wife, Colleen, who carved out a groundbreaking role for herself as Gordie's agent, promoter and business partner. In addition to their half-century-long love story, the Howes rewrote the book on how a star athlete

CONTINUED ON PAGE 39

Backhanded compliment

Back in the day when the sticks were made of wood and they weren't curved, Gordie Howe enjoyed two huge advantages: He was ambidextrous and worked extensively on his backhand. After his death, Wayne Gretzky said: "When I was 10 years old he told me, 'Make sure you work on your backhand.' So I always had great pride and scored a lot of goals because of my backhand. (A) similarity we had as players was his backhand was strong and solid, and I think that's the one thing I really picked up from him."
DETROIT FREE PRESS

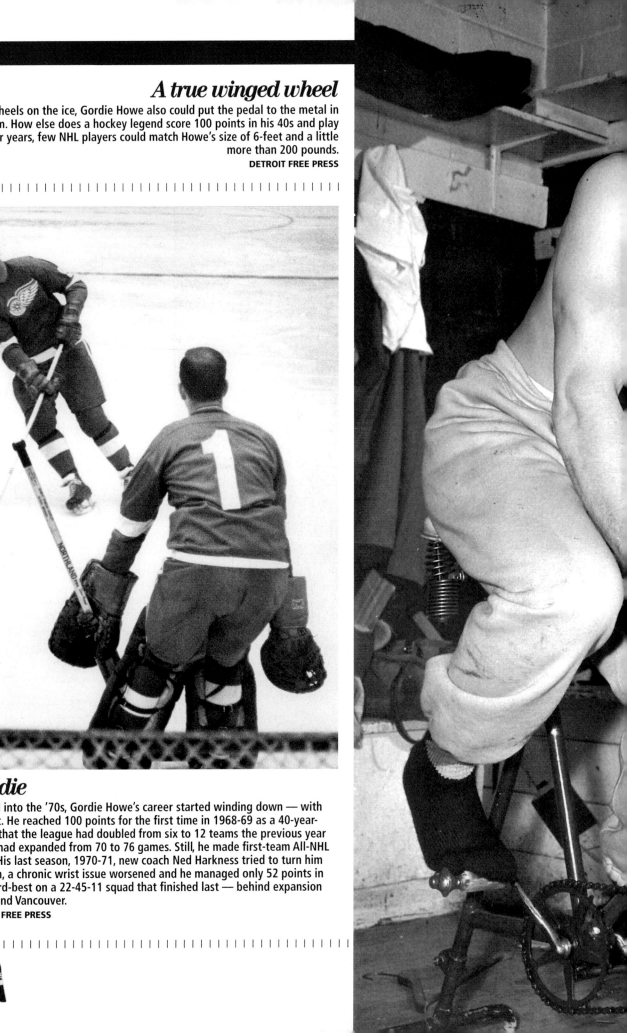

A true winged wheel

Noted for his wheels on the ice, Gordie Howe also could put the pedal to the metal in the training room. How else does a hockey legend score 100 points in his 40s and play until his 50s? For years, few NHL players could match Howe's size of 6-feet and a little more than 200 pounds.

DETROIT FREE PRESS

Golden oldie

As the '60s turned into the '70s, Gordie Howe's career started winding down — with the Wings, at least. He reached 100 points for the first time in 1968-69 as a 40-year-old. It didn't hurt that the league had doubled from six to 12 teams the previous year and the schedule had expanded from 70 to 76 games. Still, he made first-team All-NHL at 39, 40 and 41. His last season, 1970-71, new coach Ned Harkness tried to turn him into a defenseman, a chronic wrist issue worsened and he managed only 52 points in 63 games, still third-best on a 22-45-11 squad that finished last — behind expansion teams in Buffalo and Vancouver.

DICK TRIPP/DETROIT FREE PRESS

GORDIE
38
9

CONTINUED FROM PAGE 36

and his wife capitalize on stardom, even decades after his final game.

At 6-feet and a little more than 200 pounds, Howe had a lumberjack body and a Paul Bunyan reputation. He was said to sign autographs at the rate of 1,000 an hour. Fans talked about him scoring goals with either hand, how he could hit batting-practice pitches into the stands at Tiger Stadium and how he rearranged the face of a bully, Lou Fontinato, during a 1959 game that was so memorable Life magazine covered it with a three-page spread.

"Howe's punches went whop, whop, whop, just like someone chopping wood," a Red Wings teammate told the magazine.

"I never had to fight again," Howe said years later, adding that in retirement he socialized with Fontinato at the suggestion of Colleen.

The debate over who was the greatest hockey player — Howe, Wayne Gretzky, Maurice Richard, Mario Lemieux or Bobby Orr — might never end, but there is little question Howe was one of the most beloved NHL stars.

Growing up in Ontario, Gretzky idolized him and wore No. 99 on his back because Howe wore No. 9. In Quebec City, owners of a bar called GH 9 assumed the name required no explanation. In Los Angeles, producers of "The Simpsons" made an image of Howe a part of one 1992 plot, then ran his career statistics during the closing credits.

Howe's on-ice persona, like his understated personality, was subtle. He was not a water bug-like skater, as Gretzky, or a fiery competitor, like Richard. He understood the game's rhythms, and he quietly excelled at every skill it demanded, from skating to shooting. He was far more durable than any other star, and he was one of the league's strongest players, as well. Howe stopped being a fighter after he had established himself as a star, but he played with an attitude. He was famous

CONTINUED ON PAGE 40

GORDIE
39

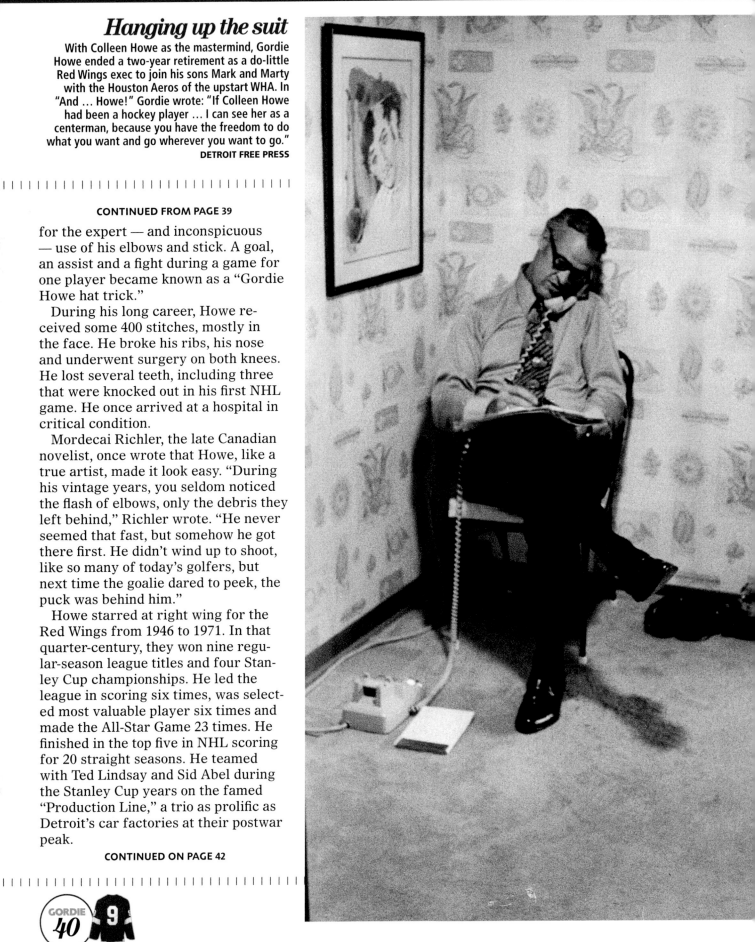

Hanging up the suit

With Colleen Howe as the mastermind, Gordie Howe ended a two-year retirement as a do-little Red Wings exec to join his sons Mark and Marty with the Houston Aeros of the upstart WHA. In "And … Howe!" Gordie wrote: "If Colleen Howe had been a hockey player … I can see her as a centerman, because you have the freedom to do what you want and go wherever you want to go."

DETROIT FREE PRESS

CONTINUED FROM PAGE 39

for the expert — and inconspicuous — use of his elbows and stick. A goal, an assist and a fight during a game for one player became known as a "Gordie Howe hat trick."

During his long career, Howe received some 400 stitches, mostly in the face. He broke his ribs, his nose and underwent surgery on both knees. He lost several teeth, including three that were knocked out in his first NHL game. He once arrived at a hospital in critical condition.

Mordecai Richler, the late Canadian novelist, once wrote that Howe, like a true artist, made it look easy. "During his vintage years, you seldom noticed the flash of elbows, only the debris they left behind," Richler wrote. "He never seemed that fast, but somehow he got there first. He didn't wind up to shoot, like so many of today's golfers, but next time the goalie dared to peek, the puck was behind him."

Howe starred at right wing for the Red Wings from 1946 to 1971. In that quarter-century, they won nine regular-season league titles and four Stanley Cup championships. He led the league in scoring six times, was selected most valuable player six times and made the All-Star Game 23 times. He finished in the top five in NHL scoring for 20 straight seasons. He teamed with Ted Lindsay and Sid Abel during the Stanley Cup years on the famed "Production Line," a trio as prolific as Detroit's car factories at their postwar peak.

CONTINUED ON PAGE 42

"During his vintage years, you seldom noticed the flash of elbows, only the debris they left behind."

MORDECAI RICHLER, Canadian novelist, on Howe's ability to play physically without drawing attention to himself

Go Green! Go Red!

Before Duffy Daugherty became a successful football coach at MSU in 1954, his lines in East Lansing were known as "Duffy's Toughies." A certain hockey player from Floral, Saskatchewan, certainly would have fit the profile. Best of all? No elbowing penalty on the gridiron.

TOM VENALECK/DETROIT FREE PRESS

CONTINUED FROM PAGE 40

Howe retired after the 1970-71 season and became a club vice president. The Wings retired his jersey in March 1972 during an elaborate ceremony at the Olympia that featured Vice President Spiro Agnew. But Howe chafed at the do-nothing role the Wings assigned him, reportedly calling it the "mushroom treatment" in which they keep you in the dark and occasionally throw manure on you. When Howe told the story, he used an earthier word than manure, and always got a laugh.

In 1973, Howe became a pro hockey player again. The Houston Aeros of the upstart World Hockey Association offered him a chance to play with sons Marty and Mark, and the Howes became stars and hockey promoters in the Sun Belt, then all three moved to the New England Whalers in 1977. When four WHA teams merged with the NHL in 1979, Howe — at 51 — started one final season.

He played in all 80 games, scoring 15 goals. Selected by coach Scotty Bowman to the 1980 All-Star Game at Detroit's new Joe Louis Arena, Howe seemed to tear up when a crowd of 21,002 gave him a 2½-minute standing ovation and chanted his name.

During his long retirement, Howe and Colleen barnstormed North America, making appearances, launching businesses, running hockey schools, publishing books and doting on their grandchildren.

He eventually became caregiver to Colleen, who suffered from Pick's disease, a rare debilitating form of dementia that included personality changes. One of the toughest men in a rugged sport fed his wife, prepared her medication and watched over her as she existed in an ever-thickening fog. She died in 2009, about a month short of their 56th wedding anniversary.

Speaking of his wife's death later that year, Howe told the Associated Press: "You can think you're a big strong guy, but if something like that happens, it

CONTINUED ON PAGE 45

A final check

Before an exhibition game in September 1970, Gordie Howe signed a two-year, $200,000 contract for his 25th and 26th seasons, which he vowed would be his last. Owner Bruce Norris declared: "When Gordie first signed with the Red Wings it was for a modest bonus and the promise of a Red Wing jacket. This time, we had to put in 400 new seats to handle his contract." Howe responded: "I've always said I've been paid satisfactorily, but not enough. I can honestly say it's quite enough this time." That night against the Rangers, Howe played a physical game, scored one goal and set up two others — as a defenseman. As it turned out, Howe soon returned to right wing, he posted his lowest point total since the 1940s, and the Wings finished dead last. Then Howe elected not to play a 26th season, despite the $100,000 lure.

DICK TRIPP/DETROIT FREE PRESS

Mrs. and Mr. Hockey

Colleen and Gordie Howe posed for this portrait in 1992, during a break at a hockey clinic in New Jersey. They met in a bowling alley in 1951 and married two years later. In "And ... Howe!" Colleen wrote: "Even though they were famous hockey players, they didn't have either the money or the opportunity to be worldly. That's why they were doing simple things like bowling at a neighborhood recreation center."
J. KYLE KEENER/DETROIT FREE PRESS

CONTINUED FROM PAGE 42

makes you weak as a kitten."

Prairie to Motor City

Born in tiny Floral, Saskatchewan, Howe grew up during the Depression in nearby Saskatoon, the sixth of nine children of Ab and Katherine Howe. Ab Howe was an American who had traveled north from Minnesota to homestead on the Canadian prairie, which was so flat that Gordie would later say you could watch your dog run away for three days.

His mother was a German immigrant who gave birth to the future Mr. Hockey in the family home after drawing water from the well and heating it, concluding the process, Howe said, by tying the umbilical cord herself.

The family struggled, sometimes eating oatmeal three times a day. Howe learned to skate and stickhandle in frozen potato patches, often using frigid horse chips for pucks. Shy, big and clumsy as a kid, his schoolmates taunted him, calling him "doughhead." But he dreamed of greater things and practiced signing his autograph at the

CONTINUED ON PAGE 47

First family of hockey

In 1965, the Howe family dressed for success in front of their house on Sunset Boulevard in Lathrup Village, Mich. From the left: Gordie (born 1928), Murray (born 1960), Colleen (born 1933), Marty (born 1954), Cathy (born 1959) and Mark (born 1955). They lived on Stawell Avenue in Detroit before moving to bigger quarters with Cathy's arrival around 1960.
HOWE FAMILY

Old Wings never fade away

Right before the 1962-63 season, the Red Wings' Production Line had a reunion of sorts, looking nothing like their famous photo in the background. Ted Lindsay (right) dropped by the team offices for the inside dope for his role as a broadcaster. Sid Abel (center) had replaced Jack Adams as the general manager a few months earlier to go with his coaching duties. And Gordie Howe was preparing for his 17th season on the ice, at age 34.

**DICK TRIPP/
DETROIT
FREE PRESS**

SID ABEL
GENERAL MANAGER

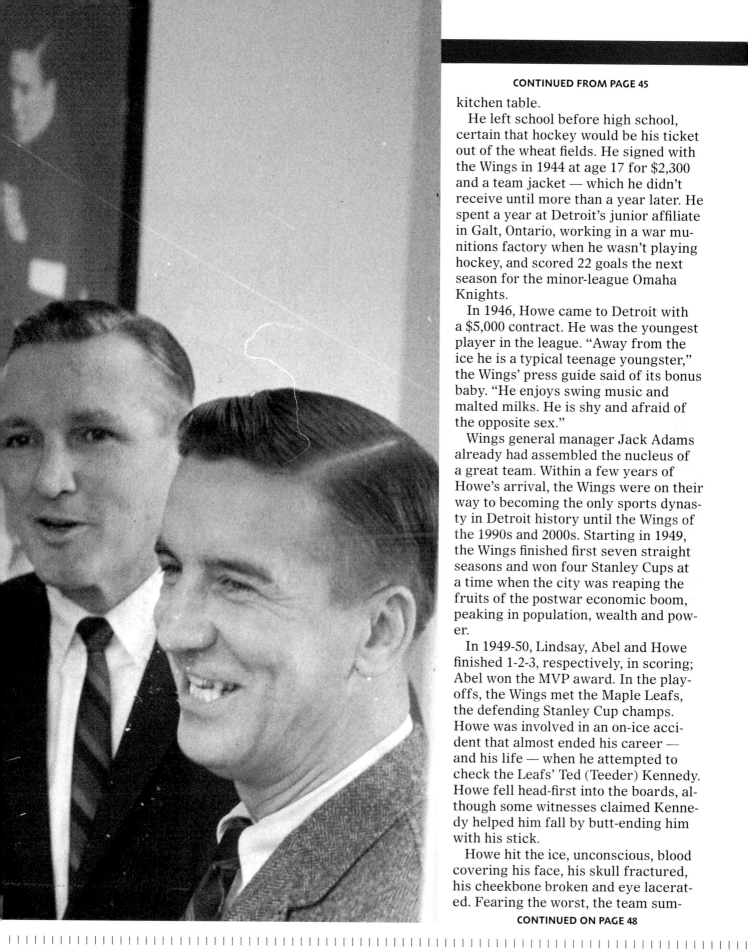

CONTINUED FROM PAGE 45

kitchen table.

He left school before high school, certain that hockey would be his ticket out of the wheat fields. He signed with the Wings in 1944 at age 17 for $2,300 and a team jacket — which he didn't receive until more than a year later. He spent a year at Detroit's junior affiliate in Galt, Ontario, working in a war munitions factory when he wasn't playing hockey, and scored 22 goals the next season for the minor-league Omaha Knights.

In 1946, Howe came to Detroit with a $5,000 contract. He was the youngest player in the league. "Away from the ice he is a typical teenage youngster," the Wings' press guide said of its bonus baby. "He enjoys swing music and malted milks. He is shy and afraid of the opposite sex."

Wings general manager Jack Adams already had assembled the nucleus of a great team. Within a few years of Howe's arrival, the Wings were on their way to becoming the only sports dynasty in Detroit history until the Wings of the 1990s and 2000s. Starting in 1949, the Wings finished first seven straight seasons and won four Stanley Cups at a time when the city was reaping the fruits of the postwar economic boom, peaking in population, wealth and power.

In 1949-50, Lindsay, Abel and Howe finished 1-2-3, respectively, in scoring; Abel won the MVP award. In the playoffs, the Wings met the Maple Leafs, the defending Stanley Cup champs. Howe was involved in an on-ice accident that almost ended his career — and his life — when he attempted to check the Leafs' Ted (Teeder) Kennedy. Howe fell head-first into the boards, although some witnesses claimed Kennedy helped him fall by butt-ending him with his stick.

Howe hit the ice, unconscious, blood covering his face, his skull fractured, his cheekbone broken and eye lacerated. Fearing the worst, the team sum-

CONTINUED ON PAGE 48

CONTINUED FROM PAGE 47

moned his family from Saskatoon. Surgeons operated to relieve the pressure on Howe's brain.

He made a quick recovery but missed the rest of the playoffs. Stirred by Howe's injury, the Wings defeated the Leafs in overtime of the seventh game and beat the New York Rangers in another seventh-game sudden death. The Olympia crowd cheered Howe, his shaved head wrapped in bandages, as he gingerly walked onto the ice to touch the Cup.

In that era, many of the Wings lived in a boarding house near Olympia run by a woman named Ma Shaw. Howe once wrote that Lindsay was "the most important presence in my life" before he married, but the friendship suffered when Howe refused to support Lindsay's attempt to organize a players' union.

And ... Howe!

As a young Red Wing, Howe was painfully introverted. Alone in the big city, he slept on a cot in the bowels of Olympia and killed rats with a hockey stick. To kill time, he would walk along Woodward Avenue, people-watching, and hang out at the Lucky Strike bowling alley on Grand River, watching people bowl.

In 1951, at the Lucky Strike, Howe met Colleen Joffa, a 17-year-old secretary who had graduated from Mackenzie High School. She had never heard of Gordie Howe. It was Gordie's first serious romance, and he was smitten.

In a letter to Colleen, which she saved, Gordie concluded, "So I'll leave you with the thought in your mind that there's a fisherman up north who is missing you like crazy. As ever, Love and all, Gord."

Colleen and Gordie eventually formed one of the most remarkable husband-wife teams in the history of professional sports. Colleen took over Gordie's business affairs and began cutting deals in the 1950s. At one time or another, the Howes owned a restaurant, a hockey arena, a travel agency, 350 head of pedigreed cattle, apartment buildings, a herd of llamas and a firm selling silo preservative.

They produced award-winning hockey instructional videos, published several books, sold life insurance, managed a platoon of hundreds of Amway distributors and started a charitable foundation. She registered as trademarks the names Mr. Hockey, Mrs. Hockey and Gordie Howe.

Howe and other former players filed a lawsuit in the early 1990s that charged the league had shortchanged them over pension benefits. In 1994, the players won a ruling in the Canadian courts that the NHL had to put $32.6 million back into the pension fund for players who retired before 1982. As a young star, Howe made little money; early in his career, he hauled cement bags in the summer. In "Net Worth," an authoritative 1991 book, authors David Cruise and Alison Griffiths asserted that Howe's reluctance to demand more from the Wings made him the most underpaid player in the history of professional sports and helped keep the salaries of other hockey players well below those in other major league sports.

When he was suing the league, Howe recognized the irony that he had refused to join the nascent players' union in the 1950s. Howe's membership would have boosted the union's status, but he was afraid of alienating Adams, the Wings' paternalistic general manager.

Cruise and Griffiths wrote: "It is a measure of how genuine was Howe's humility, off-ice geniality and love of hockey, that he isn't the most hated man of his era."

Not all of the Howes' off-ice business adventures were successful. Colleen once said they lost the equivalent of a life savings in the cattle herd, and a $90-million real estate project in Brighton, Mich., that was to include a hotel, condos and four ice arenas never got

CONTINUED ON PAGE 50

Baby Boomers

By the end of the 1950s, Colleen and Gordie Howe nearly had their quartet of children for the First Family of Hockey. From the left: Marty Gordon, Mark Steven and Cathleen Jill. The future doctor, Murray, would join the brood in 1960.
DETROIT FREE PRESS

GORDIE
48 9

CONTINUED FROM PAGE 48

off the ground.

A legend's final lap

After the death of Colleen and even after Howe began showing symptoms of dementia himself, he toured North America, raising millions for Alzheimer's research. In recent years he spent time with his children and grandchildren, went ocean fishing, hit golf balls, walked and raked leaves — sometimes for hours. But he often could not remember the next day what he had done.

On Dec. 31, 2013, Howe seemed disoriented and unsteady on the ice before a Wings-Leafs alumni game at Comerica Park, where he joined Lindsay to drop the ceremonial first pucks as the crowd chanted "Gor-die! Gordie!" Ten months later, Putnam published his most recent autobiography, "Mr. Hockey: My Story," which would sell extremely well. However, within two weeks of the book's release, Howe suffered a severe stroke at his daughter Cathy's home in Lubbock, Texas, and for a time seemed near death. As the family rushed to his bedside, son Murray, a doctor specializing in radiology, told the Free Press: "I feel like this is his final lap around the rink."

But Howe rallied and, eventually, his children helped arrange for him to travel to Tijuana, Mexico, for a stem-cell treatment not permitted in the United States. Howe's rally accelerated, which drew headlines beyond the sports pages across the country, although some skeptics politely questioned the ethics and long-term efficacy of such "medical tourism."

In February 2015, looking frail and saying little, Howe nonetheless journeyed to his hometown of Saskatoon and received a hero's welcome at a celebrity dinner in his honor. One of the stars in attendance, Gretzky, recalled meeting Howe in 1972, when No. 99 was a towheaded preteen sensation. A famous photo showed Howe playfully hooking Gretzky with his stick.

Aisle 9?

Despite his severe stroke in October 2014, Gordie Howe regained his ability to walk and relished pushing the cart at Kroger while grocery shopping with his son Murray. He did so until a few weeks before his death.
HOWE FAMILY

"We were standing there, Gordon grabbed his stick, actually put it around my throat," Gretzky told reporters at the event. "It went on to be one of the most popular pictures I've ever signed."

As late as the spring of 2016, Howe would accompany Murray for excursions in and around Toledo. A favorite outing was shopping at a local Kroger, where Howe would push the cart. Murray also described the breakfast his father consumed daily: four eggs, toast with butter, a banana, four sausage links and a bowl of oatmeal.

Howe's last visit to the Joe came on March 28, a few days before his 88th

CONTINUED ON PAGE 53

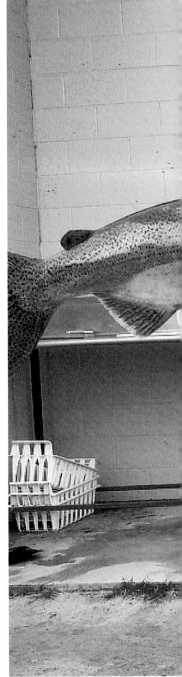

Fish, be afraid

Rival players weren't the only ones who should have cowered with Gordie Howe nearby. Fish should have, too. Marty, Gordie and Mark showed off their impressive haul during the Red Wings' training camp in Traverse City, Mich., in September 2013.
HOWE FAMILY

Fishin' buddies

Right before his father's 86th birthday in 2014, Mark Howe acknowledged Mr. Hockey's issues with dementia but wanted to accentuate the many positives in Gordie's life. "We try to make it fun for Dad, and that means fishing," Mark said. "He always loved and still loves fishing."
HOWE FAMILY

Destination Houston

The word came down on May 31, 1973, to Gordie Howe and the Red Wings that NHL president Clarence Campbell would not allow Mark, 18, and Marty, 19, to play for the team. The league had agreed in 1967 with the Canadian Amateur Hockey Association not to draft anyone under 20. Campbell's decision all but guaranteed Howe's sons would sign with the WHA's Houston Aeros. Howe, at age 45, now needed to decide whether to come out of retirement to join them. Campell said it would be "a tragedy" if Howe switched leagues. "The prestige of the NHL will suffer without the Howe name," said Jim Bishop, the Wings' executive vice president.

ALAN R. KAMUDA/
DETROIT FREE PRESS

High on life

A few days from the one-year anniversary of Gordie Howe's stroke, son Murray spoke at the Troy Community Coalition Celebrity Night Dinner and brought him along. He shook hands, gave hugs and glowed. "It juices him up," Murray said. "He loves being Mr. Hockey."
SALWAN GEORGES/DETROIT FREE PRESS

CONTINUED FROM PAGE 50

birthday. He mugged with players in the dressing room. He stood tall as he received a birthday cake during a break in the action. And he enjoyed the fans' rendition of "Happy Birthday."

Howe would make a few more public appearances, but his health began to deteriorate again as the cold, wet days of spring transitioned into the longer, warmer days of a traditional, fabulous Michigan summer. On June 10, a Friday, Murray sent this text to the Free Press: "Mr. Hockey left this morning peacefully, beautifully, and with no regrets." And Wings owner Mike Ilitch issued this statement: "Today is a sad day for the Detroit Red Wings and the entire hockey world as together we mourn the loss of one of the greatest hockey players of all time. There is no nickname more fitting for him than Mr. Hockey. ... It is truly a blessing to have had him both in our organization and our city for so many years."

The death of Gordie, after the passing of Colleen, brought to a close a unique chapter in Detroit sports history. The Howes were unrivaled: The modest star from the Canadian prairies and the hard-driving dealmaker from Detroit.

Once, at a dinner, Gordie was talking in his usual, self-deprecating way when Colleen interrupted.

"Gordie, don't talk with your hands in front of your mouth," she said.

"Dear, don't give me orders," he responded. "People will get the wrong impression that you're the boss."

There was no acrimony in the exchange, just tenderness and a little irony. Their children said they still held hands in their 70s when they walked on the beach or attended a movie.

"It's been a mutual agreement, a partnership," Gordie said. "I married a strong lady who has been very, very good for me because there are a lot of departments where I know I lack."

The best medicine?

Controversial treatment may have given Gordie two more years with his family

ROBIN ERB & GEORGE SIPPLE

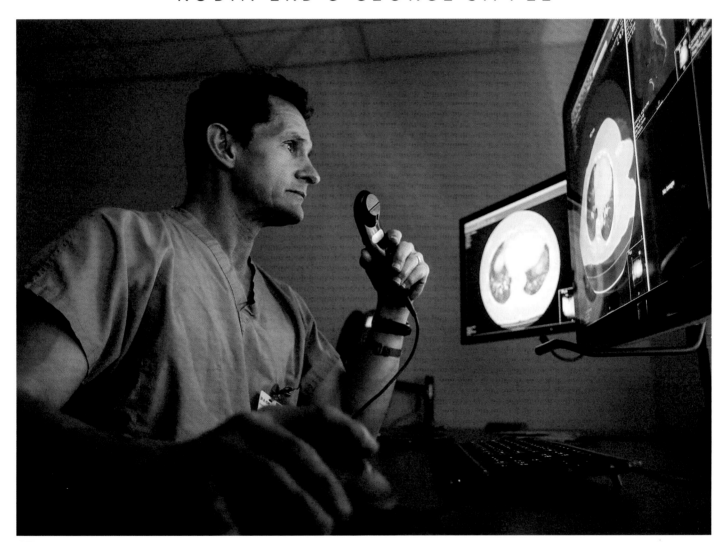

The good doctor

Like older brothers Marty and Mark, Murray Howe played hockey growing up and even played on a Toronto junior team with Wayne Gretzky. But Howe couldn't make the Michigan Wolverines — and eventually transitioned to medicine. "I have absolutely no excuses for why I wasn't very good, other than, I just was not very good," Howe told the Toledo Blade with a wry smile in 2013. "On the same team with Gretzky, he was the best … and I was the worst."

RYAN GARZA/DETROIT FREE PRESS

ook, he gets it — the skepticism over what seemed to be his father's medical miracle, says Gordie Howe's youngest son.

But Dr. Murray Howe, head of sports medicine imaging at ProMedica Toledo Hospital, also says he knows what he saw: The once-powerful Mr. Hockey — his father — struck mute and unable to walk by a stroke on Oct. 26, 2014. Who by Dec. 1 "was nearly catatonic."

A family that had accepted his final days. They had made funeral plans.

And a Tijuana medical clinic where, on Dec. 8, the elder Howe sat straight up in bed just hours after an injection of about 100 million stem cells and demanded with an astonishingly strong voice that he needed to use the restroom.

"He says, 'I'll walk,' and I said, 'You can't walk,'" Murray Howe recalled. "He says, 'The hell I can't.' And he sits up and puts his feet over the side of the bed and stood up. If I hadn't been there and seen that happen with my dad, I don't know if I'd believe it either."

Fans rejoiced over the Christmastime news. But the medical establishment was beyond skeptical.

Some doctors called the procedure in Mexico — a two-step injection of two types of stem cells — questionable at best and a scam at worst. They criticized the providers of the procedure for giving the treatment for free to a Hall of Fame legend but charging others $20,000 or more — all in the name of research. And they accused Dr. Murray Howe in particular — a doctor trained at one of the nation's most prestigious medical schools, the University of Michigan — of raising false hopes.

"There is no scientific evidence at present that the kind of procedures that he was reported to have received … have efficacy in stroke. That is the bottom line," wrote Judy Illes, director of the National Core for Neuroethics and a medical genetics professor at the University of British Columbia. Dr. David Gorski, a Wayne State University professor and a breast cancer doctor at the Barbara Ann Karmanos Cancer Institute in Detroit, was among the first to raise red flags, writing about it at the medical blog Science-based Medicine.

The clinic the Howes went to was operated by Tijuana-based Novastem and supplied with stem cells by San Diego-based Stemedica, which also supplied stem cells to four clinical trials within the U.S.

Howe, already struggling with advancing dementia at 86, was paralyzed on his right side after the stroke. He could no longer talk or walk on his own. His 200-pound frame had withered to 170 or so as his ability to swallow deteriorated. His legs were skin on bone. Oldest son Marty Howe said: "It was like he was turning invisible."

In February 2015, Murray said his father now "feeds himself, he can help folding laundry. He can walk about a half-mile. … Sometimes he's a little bit wobbly on his feet. He calls himself Wobbly Wilbur. But he'll shake it off and get a little dance in his step and he'll be fine."

Skeptics of the stem-cell treatment were quick to point out a number of other possible reasons for Gordie's rally: Rehydration, the body's natural ability to repair itself after stroke, and a placebo effect that renews a will to live.

Murray acknowledged: A single anecdote fell far short of scientific proof of cure. "All I'm doing," he said, "is sharing with the world my experience of what I saw with my father."

Comments like that didn't silence Murray's critics. Nor did an interview with USA TODAY in which he said: "Of course it was stem cells, because how else do you explain it? It wasn't placebo effect because my father's short-term memory is so poor. He didn't remember he had a stroke, and he didn't remember he had treatment for a stroke to get better."

The Howes returned to Mexico in June 2015 for additional stem-cell treatment.

A month before Gordie's death, Murray appeared at a news conference announcing that a clinical trial for patients with traumatic brain injuries would be conducted at Toledo Hospital using Stemedica's stem cells. The research effort would be called the Gordie Howe TBI Initiative.

"If I hadn't been there and seen that happen with my dad, I don't know if I'd believe it either."

DR. MURRAY HOWE, on Gordie's fight to walk again after receiving an injection of stem cells

'Hockey is a

ON HIS SECRET TO STAYING PRODUCTIVE DURING 25 YEARS WITH THE RED WINGS: "There is no doubt in my mind that it was my love for the game. To succeed, you've got to love what you're doing. I tell kids, 'If you don't love it, get out of the way for someone who does.'"

ON HIS TOUGH PLAY: "I learned to play religious hockey. That is, it's better to give than to receive."

ON WHETHER HE REGRETTED HIS AGGRESSIVE BEHAVIOR: "No, not really. When I was young I was told you have to protect yourself. I just wanted to be square with the bugs. If somebody got me, I wanted to get them back."

ON HIS OFF-ICE KINDNESS: "I remember how excited I was as a kid when I got an autograph. Once I asked my hero, Ab Welsh of the Saskatoon Quakers, for an autograph. He took me into the room, had the other players sign my book and then he gave me his stick. God, I slept with that thing when I got home. I told Mom, 'If I'm going to be a hockey player, I better learn how to write.' I wasted a lot of paper practicing autographs."

ON HOW HE COPED WITH HIS WIFE COLLEEN'S STRUGGLE WITH PICK'S DISEASE: "You do it with help. I didn't realize how many other people had troubles like this until they started phoning me from all over the world."

ON A CAREER-DEFINING MOMENT AS A MINOR-LEAGUER IN OMAHA: "I played very little. But one time, one of our teammates was having a real problem, and I jumped on the ice and took on the man that was fighting him. Those days, there was no helmets and I was kind of a crazy man anyway, so I bumped his head on the ice. That was the end of the fight. I came off and Tommy Ivan said, 'What's the matter? Don't you like him?' I said, 'I don't like anyone out here.' Well, I ended up taking the position of the guy that I fought for. I had one or two goals up until then, before Christmas, and then I scored

20-something after. Later, I asked (Ivan), 'Did that statement have anything to do with why you played me?' He said, 'No. Everything.'"

ON HIS NHL DEBUT AS AN 18-YEAR-OLD ON OCT. 16, 1946: "My mind was full of simple little thoughts that day. I remember thinking, 'If I could hang on, at least I could say I played for a year.'"

ON HIS FIRST GOAL, AT 13:39 OF SECOND PERIOD AGAINST TORONTO IN HIS NHL DEBUT: "Adam Brown was on the left, Sid (Abel) on the right. It must have been a good exchange because I ended up on the left wing, to the right of the goaltender. The puck came across — it was either a pass or it was deflected — but it came to me. I saw it in front of me, and half the net was open. I was about 10 feet out. It went halfway up."

ON HIS FAMOUS NO. 9: "I was No. 17 for two seasons. It started in Omaha because I was 17 years of age, so I became No. 17 up here. But then the trainer came to me and said, 'Conacher just got traded to New York. No. 9 is open. Do you want it?' I said, 'No.' He said, 'It will get you a lower berth on the train.' I said, 'I'll take it.' That's how I became No. 9."

ON HIS SPORT: "Hockey is a man's game."

ON THE PRICE YOU HAVE TO PAY, TO SPORTS ILLUSTRATED IN 1964: "I had 50 stitches in my face one year. That was a bad year. I only got 10 stitches last year. That was a good year."

ON SUCCESS: "You find that you have peace of mind and can enjoy yourself, get more sleep and rest when you know that it was 100% effort that you gave, win or lose."

ON HIS EYES MISTING AS HE RECALLED THE OLD TIMES AND HIS OLD TEAMMATES: "I can tell you, some of the best moments in your life can feel like yesterday. But others, they can feel like a long time ago."

On who wears the pants ...

In "And ... Howe!" Gordie wrote: "People have asked me if I ever felt Colleen was too much in control. ... It's hard to feel that way when I know that Colleen does 80 or 90% of the work for our family and business. It's strange they ask me that question when I'm out playing golf, and Colleen is at home in the office, doing every possible task."

SUSAN TUSA/DETROIT FREE PRESS

GORDIE **9**

56

man's game'

The great debate

Who was the best ever? Orr and The Great One vote Gordie

GENE MYERS

Gordie Howe's death unleashed a torrent of compliments from all corners of the hockey world. But it also reignited the old debate of which player was the best in hockey history.

Before Howe hit his prime, that label usually belonged to Montreal right wing Maurice (Rocket) Richard. In 1963, Howe passed Richard as the NHL's all-time leading goal-scorer with No. 545 — and then added 256 more before his career ended in 1980. (And that didn't include his 174 goals in six WHA seasons, which the NHL refused to recognize.) He also had 1,049 NHL assists (334 in the WHA) and won the Hart Trophy six times as league MVP (once in the WHA, at age 46).

Howe was so universally regarded as the best ever that he wasn't just known as Mr. Hockey. His other nicknames included The King of Hockey, The Legend, The Great Gordie, Power, The Most and Mr. All-Star.

A contender for the title emerged in the late 1960s and early '70s, Bobby Orr, a revolutionary defenseman for Boston who would carry the puck end-to-end, deliver passes, score goals and still anchor the backend because he could skate like the wind. Orr played only nine full seasons because of chronic knee troubles, but he won eight Norris trophies as the top defenseman and three Hart trophies. He averaged 1.4 points a game and in 1970-71 posted 139 points with 37 goals and 102 assists. His plus-124 rating that season had never been topped; in fact, Orr had three of the top-10 plus-minus seasons in history. (Gretzky had one, No. 3; the stat wasn't kept during nearly all of Howe's career, but his son Mark ranked No. 8, at plus-85 in 1985-86).

Another contender started to emerge in 1979-80, Howe's final NHL season and the first for Wayne Gretzky, a revolutionary center for Edmonton who would deliver seeing-eye passes, score seemingly at will, and shatter records and win awards faster than a speeding slapshot. Gretzky, growing up in Brantford, Ontario, loved the Red Wings and idolized Howe, who would befriend him throughout his career, starting as a 10-year-old. Gretzky finished with 894 goals, 1,963 assists and nine Hart trophies, including eight straight from 1980-87.

Who really should be considered hockey's GOAT — greatest of all time? A popular compromise went this way: Howe was the most complete player, because he could score, defend and provide muscle. Gretzky was the greatest offensive force. And Orr was the greatest

CONTINUED ON PAGE 59

CONTINUED FROM PAGE 58

game-changer, unlike any player past or future.

But, for the public record, Gretzky and Orr repeatedly declared Howe as the greatest.

Orr, growing up in Parry Sound, Ontario, considered Howe a childhood idol, too. In a 2003 interview with Bill Dow for the Free Press, Orr said: "Are you at your computer? Go to mrhockey.com and just look at the numbers. Remember, he played against all the talent in the Original Six era when they were traveling by train, no char-

ters. In 1968-69, he had 103 points. It was his best season, and he was 41 years old. In his last year at age 52, he played all 80 games and scored 15 goals with 26 assists. When it comes to who was the best hockey player ever, don't even go there with me." He chuckled. "There is no question that Gordie is the best of all time."

In Howe's last autobiography, "Mr. Hockey: My Story," released a few weeks before his 2014 stroke, Orr wrote in the foreword: "Many times over the years, I have been asked who I consider

Fancy meeting you here, Mr. Hockey

In January 1984, Gordie Howe, in one of his many promotional gigs, this time for cargo airline Emery Worldwide, dropped by the Joe to present the Emery Edge Award, given to the player on each team with the top plus-minus rating. (John Ogrodnick led the Wings with a plus-11 in 1982-83.) Fans were riveted watching Howe converse with Wayne Gretzky, a 22-year-old Edmonton sensation already with four straight MVP awards. In 1983-84, Gretzky would win his fifth of eight straight Hart trophies, record 208 points (73 goals, 135 assists) and post a plus-98 rating. **MARY SCHROEDER/DETROIT FREE PRESS**

to be the greatest hockey player of all time. My answer has never changed — it is Gordie Howe."

In Detroit for Howe's visitation and funeral, Gretzky called Howe the greatest in countless interviews. The Great One, Gretzky's nickname, closed an emotional night in February 2015 when Howe traveled to Saskatoon, Saskatchewan, for the final time, to be honored by his hometown. "He is, he was, he will always be the greatest of all time," Gretzky declared in words that were not rehearsed. An hour afterward, he told ESPN.com: "It was from the heart. You don't plan something like that. He's so special."

Sixteen months later, in the national spotlight after Howe's passing, Gretzky said in the Motor City: "He was the greatest player ever. I say this all the time: Bobby Orr and Gordie Howe, pick who you think is better. I happen to be a little biased because I was a forward. I'll take Gordie. But more importantly, he was the nicest man I ever met."

An unbiased opinion? Stan Fischler, the best-known hockey historian, told the Free Press' Mitch Albom that — simply, hands down, no doubt about it — Howe was "top of the list … the top."

It's a dog's life

Even a dog would have wanted to watch the 2002 Stanley Cup-winning Red Wings! That team featured future Hall of Famers Chris Chelios, Sergei Fedorov, Dominik Hasek, Brett Hull, Igor Larionov, Nicklas Lidstrom, Luc Robitaille, Brendan Shanahan and Steve Yzerman; a coach already in the Hockey Hall of Fame, Scotty Bowman; and a dazzling Russian rookie, Pavel Datsyuk. Before the Wings' second-round series against the Blues, Gordie Howe brought his dog to Joe Louis Arena for a visit, which included watching practice from the Zamboni entrance.
JULIAN H. GONZALEZ/ DETROIT FREE PRESS

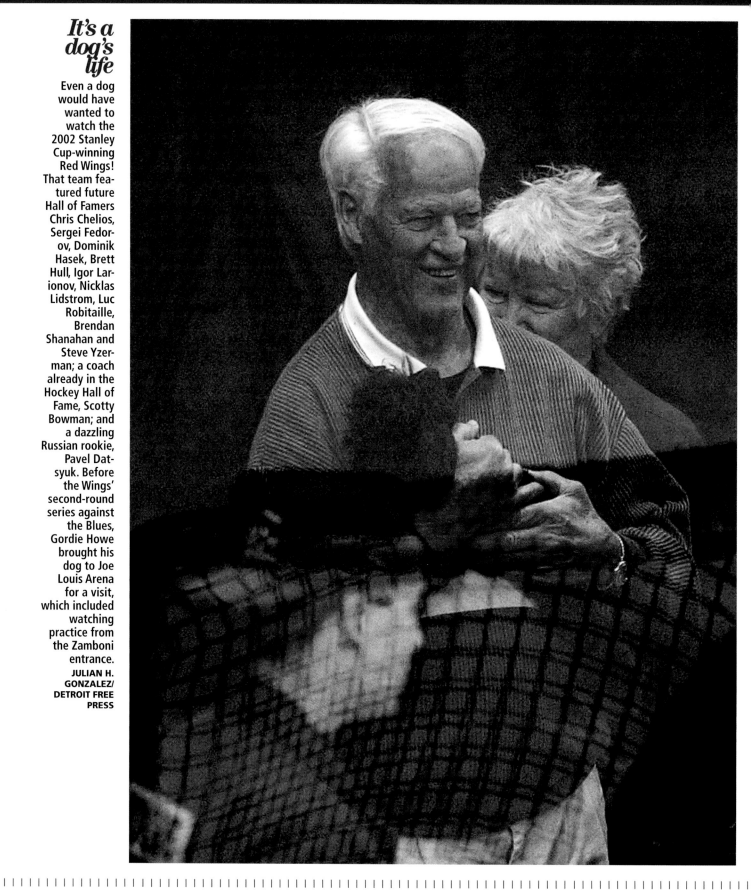

Reporters share their memories of Mr. Hockey

What Gordie meant to us

A doggone good question

CARLOS MONARREZ

I once saved Gordie Howe during an awards dinner.

In 2001, when my wife worked for a business I shall refer to only as "another newspaper in Detroit," Howe and his wife, Colleen, were being honored at a fancy dinner.

There were other honorees, like Detroit Mayor Dennis Archer. But my wife and I sat with the Howes and their incredibly tiny and polite dog, who cuddled almost invisibly in Colleen's lap the entire dinner. (Yes, they brought a dog to a fancy restaurant. And who was going to tell Mr. Hockey he couldn't do that?)

I had moved to Detroit in 1999 after growing up in Los Angeles a rabid Kings fan. The only thing I really knew about Howe was that he was a legend and Wayne Gretzky spoke of him and the Red Wings' Production Line the way a literary scholar discusses Norse saga.

But there I was. At a table with a legend. And the legend didn't seem all that comfortable.

There were about 10 of us at the table and everyone tried to make small talk with the Howes, who were polite and gracious. But Gordie was also a farm boy from Saskatchewan and small talk didn't come easy, at least on this night while sitting mostly with egg-head newspaper editors.

No one knew it at the time, but Colleen was in the early stages of Pick's disease, a rare form of dementia, which would claim her life in 2009. Gordie seemed a little nervous and the Howes were mostly quiet during dinner.

I've always been wary of talking shop with athletes and celebrities, unsure of how much they enjoy their fame and reliving their glory. But I had to ask about the dog, who had turned into the elephant in the room. Everyone was pretending he didn't exist, but I couldn't resist and had to ask his name.

"Rocket," Gordie said.

"After Maurice Richard?" I asked.

Gordie's face lit up as if he had just scored a hat trick.

Just like that, I saved Gordie from an evening of awkward silence. We spoke the same language and soon we were chatting about The Rocket and the Canadiens, about Ted Lindsay and Alex Delvecchio, about Terry Sawchuk and Jacques Plante, and about the Original Six.

I ran into Howe a few times over the years at various Red Wings events. He didn't remember me and I didn't expect him to. But I guess I can always say I once gave Gordie Howe an assist.

'Gordie Howe had

Truly a never-ending source of joy

HELENE ST. JAMES

My great good fortune includes covering the Detroit Red Wings back when Gordie Howe would make regular appearances in the locker room.

I was waiting to interview a player, and suddenly there he was, right next to me. He looked at me, laughed, and teased "no girls allowed." Then we chatted for a few minutes.

Seeing Howe around Joe Louis Arena was such a joy. It was fun to watch players new to the team approach him. There was such reverence for him, but he couldn't have been more down-to-earth.

You just knew if you talked to him, you would end up laughing at some point. He told stories with such animation, you never wanted the tales to have an ending.

As great a player as Howe was, I don't think there's a better tribute than how many people have a cherished memory of him.

Every time I've written about him, my inbox floods with people sharing a story of meeting him — at a rink, in a parking lot, in an airport, anywhere. Always the memory is fond, always the interaction reveals Gordie Howe had time for everyone.

A classy ambassador for the sport

JEFF SEIDEL

People fell in love with hockey because of Gordie Howe.

That is Howe's legacy.

He was a great player and an even better man.

An ambassador for the sport. An ambassador for Detroit.

Classy. Kind. And full of integrity.

All the people he touched.

The people who saw him play. The people he met on the streets or in restaurants and across the state. And the thousands of hockey players that he inspired.

It's hard to find somebody who doesn't have a Gordie Howe story in Hockeytown.

Maybe, it's just how he inspired them. Or how much they appreciated them.

But so many others have personal stories about him.

Walk into any rink in Michigan, as the hockey community forever mourned his loss, and it didn't take long to hear a Gordie Howe story.

Gordie Howe was hockey royalty but acted like a common man.

A king who took off his skates and lived outside the palace.

He was one of us. The best of us.

time for everyone.'

A fighter all the way to the end

DREW SHARP

One of the life lessons learned during an impoverished childhood in the throes of the Great Depression was self-sufficiency, doing whatever necessary to get the job done. Gordie Howe applied those same principles on the ice. If subtlety didn't work, Howe delivered a not-so-subtle elbow to the head to get across the message. Nobody could move him off the puck. And if you tried, brace yourself for the impending punishment.

Howe nearly died in 1950 after fracturing his skull in the playoffs. But such a scare didn't deter him.

There was a veneer of physical indestructibility, making the news of Howe's death rather surprising. We were prepared for this late in October 2014, when word first broke about his health crisis after a stroke.

That Howe survived another 20 months only added to the already storied legend of the greatest hockey player who ever breathed. Death might finally have won one of its toughest fights ever. But Howe didn't surrender meekly, even enjoying a recovery through experimental foreign stem-cell treatments that even his family thought bordered on miraculous.

Detroit has been graced with many great athletes, but only two could anyone honestly classify as the greatest in their respective fields during their careers — Howe and boxer Joe Louis.

Wayne Gretzky — the Great One — who wore No. 99 in honor of Howe's No. 9 called Howe the greatest hockey player ever.

All you had to say was "Mr. Hockey."

Prone to random acts of kindness

GEORGE SIPPLE

Gordie Howe will certainly be remembered for his 801 goals and 1,850 NHL points.

He will be remembered for the hat trick that bears his name — a goal, an assist and a fight in the same game.

He will be remembered for six Hart trophies as the NHL's most valuable player, six Art Ross trophies as the league's leading scorer and four Stanley Cups.

He played 25 of his 26 NHL seasons with the Detroit Red Wings, but some will remember him for his time in the old World Hockey Association, skating with his sons, and for all the different decades that he managed to play in.

I will remember Gordie Howe mostly for his kindness.

There were many times over the years that I ran into Howe at Joe Louis Arena before Wings games. He usually would acknowledge me with a smile, a nod or a quick remark as he passed by in the press box.

One of my favorite memories was an elevator ride with Howe and a few fans before a game. Howe noticed a young boy carrying a mini-hockey stick. The boy, seemingly unaware of who Howe was, bristled when Mr. Hockey asked to see him shoot.

The boy's father, well aware of how lucky his son was to interact with a hockey legend, prodded the boy to do as asked. When the boy did not, Howe playfully delivered an elbow to the boy's chest and turned and grinned toward everyone else in the elevator.

I laughed because the boy seemed clueless as to why his father was so excited.

"He is soft-spoken, self-deprecating and thoughtful. He is also one of the most vicious, cruel and mean men I ever met in a hockey game."

**AN UNIDENTIFIED RIVAL PLAYER, IN A WINGS
COMMEMORATIVE PROGRAM FOR HOWE'S FINAL SEASON**

SCOTTY BOWMAN, HALL OF FAME COACH: "The best part of Gordie's game was his toughness. The space he created enabled him to be the player he was."

FRANK MAHOVLICH, HALL OF FAME LEFT WING AND FORMER TEAMMATE: "No matter if it was an exhibition game or a playoff game, everyone came to see him play. He was a beautiful skater with a great shot, and he was so strong in the corners. The man was so gifted. But he was also very wonderful with the fans whenever they would meet him."

KEITH MAGNUSON, FORMER BLACK-HAWKS TOUGH GUY: "I also grew up in Saskatoon, and after I met him as a 10-year-old, he became my hero and the inspiration for pursuing a hockey career. But when I played against him for

CONTINUED ON PAGE 67

Scrapbook

Gordie Howe certainly looked like a fresh-faced newcomer when he made the Red Wings as an 18-year-old rookie in 1946. He played in 58 of the 60 games, recording seven goals and 15 assists for 22 points (ninth on the team) and notching 52 penalty minutes (fifth). At 22-27-11, the Wings finished fourth and lost in the playoffs to Toronto in five games. Howe didn't score in his first postseason — but did lead the Wings with 18 penalty minutes.

PHOTO ILLUSTRATION BY J. KYLE KEENER/ DETROIT FREE PRESS

"It was an honor to wear the same uniform, spend time with, laugh, joke and seek advice from him. Gordie's humility and kindness left a permanent impression on me, greatly influencing how I tried to conduct myself throughout my career."

CONTINUED FROM PAGE 65

the first time, I wanted to see how tough he really was. I took a really good run at him but it was like hitting a cement wall. He didn't even move, but I went down on one knee and got up quickly. As I skated down the ice, I quickly found myself up in the air. Gordie had stuck his stick between my blade and boot and just kind of threw me into the corner."

STAN MIKITA, HALL OF FAME CENTER, ABOUT THE TIME HE "ACCIDENTALLY" CUT HOWE UNDER AN EYE: "A couple of months later at the Olympia we were both turning in the Wings' end. The next thing I remember I was at the Chicago bench, my head is killing me. Our backup goalie, Denis DeJordy, said he was the only one in the building who saw what happened. Gordie had skated by me, slipped his right hand up under his armpit, pulled out his fist, popped me in the jaw and put his glove back on. A few shifts later he ambled by and asked if I learned anything. I said, 'Are we even?' Gordie says, 'I'll think about it.'"

BRAD PARK, HALL OF FAME DEFENSEMAN: "Gordie went out of his way to introduce rookies to his lifestyle. In Detroit one night he threw an elbow at me and I went under it and put him down. Before I knew it, I saw his stick coming at me like he was going to take my teeth out. Instead, he got me in the Adam's apple and I went down for the count. Gordie was determined to protect his livelihood. But today he couldn't play because with all the cameras, he'd be suspended all the time. But God, he's just a wonderful guy."

STAN FISCHLER, HOCKEY HISTORIAN: "He could shoot, pass, skate, stickhandle, check and fight as well as or better than anyone."

GLENN HALL, HALL OF FAME GOALTENDER: "He was very, very deceptive, so you never knew where he was going to shoot. Gordie was so smart around the net. When a shot was coming from the point, instead of interfering heavy, he would often just pull down the top of my stick, lifting my blade off the ice."

MAGNUSON AGAIN: Howe "went around a defenseman, holding him off with one hand, and with the other he fired the puck one-handed past Esposito. I swear that thing had the velocity of a two-handed shot. Tony never expected that, and no one in the building could believe it."

NEIL ARMSTRONG, HALL OF FAME LINESMAN: "Gordie always had time for people, even in the opposing rinks."

HOWE FAMILY, STATEMENT AFTER MR. HOCKEY'S DEATH: "Gordie truly loved his fans and spending time in the public life. As a family, we always said that he was at his best when he was around others. Whether it was giving a young aspiring hockey player an 'elbow' for a photograph pose or pranking a fan by pretending to sign someone's forehead, he relished the opportunity to be around those who loved him. His smile and genuine care for others was infectious and inspired us all."

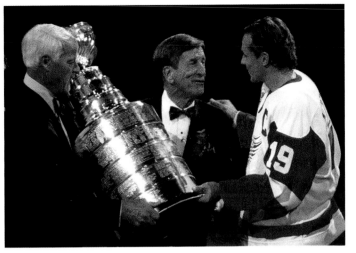

Passing the torch

In 1997, the Red Wings ended a 42-year Stanley Cup drought. On opening night for the next season, Gordie Howe and Ted Lindsay from that '55 team presented the Cup to captain Steve Yzerman. Amid the cheers, Yzerman smiled and told Howe: "Thanks for coming."
JULIAN H. GONZALEZ/DFP

ELLIOTT TRUMBULL, WINGS PR DIRECTOR FROM 1958-65: "It was a privilege to work with Gordie during my seven seasons with the Red Wings, and it was an honor to call him a dear friend for the past 56 years. As I wrote in my last note to him, 'You were the greatest, you are the greatest, and you always will be.'"

HALL AGAIN: "He was the greatest player to have ever played the game. No one has ever been better because he was the total player. He was the best scorer, the toughest hockey player, and he knew there were two ends in the rink. He would come back to his own end to check, which none of the big scorers really do. He played the game the way it should have been played. They talk about his elbows and everything else, but I never saw him elbow anybody unless they tried to take his puck. It was his puck and everybody should know that. He protected himself the way he should. I always say Bobby Orr was just a hair beneath Gordie, but Bobby was finished at age 29, where Gordie played until he was like 89."

BRUCE MARTYN, RED WINGS RADIO PLAY-BY-PLAY VOICE FROM 1964-95: "I have been asked 100 times who was the greatest, Howe or Wayne Gretzky, and I can tell you that Gordie was the best all-around hockey player I have ever seen. Gretzky, of course, was a great offensive hockey player. I've told everybody, you take five Wayne Gretzkys and I'll take five Gordie Howes and let's have a game. He never needed a protector like Gretzky did, he played both ways, he skated as well as anybody, he scored goals, he did everything and he was toughest guy in the league."

MARTYN AGAIN: "Gordie also protected the whole team. We used to play in Toronto on Saturday when there were just six teams in the league and then we'd take the train to Detroit for the Sunday night game. If something happened to a Wings player on Saturday night in Toronto, you could just look for the perpetrator because when he went into the boards with Gordie the other guy would be bleeding. He was very, very quiet, that is probably why he wasn't captain or a coach. He just led by example."

HOWIE MEEKER, TORONTO RIGHT WING, ON HOWE'S HIT ON SYL APPS IN HIS 1946 NHL DEBUT: "When the game was half over, we were saying, 'Hey, the big hayseed on the right wing is going to be a hell of a hockey player.'"

RED WINGS 1946-47 MEDIA GUIDE, ON THE 18-YEAR-OLD ROOKIE FROM SASKATOON: "Away from the ice he is a typical

CONTINUED ON PAGE 68

BARACK OBAMA, 44TH PRESIDENT OF THE UNITED STATES:

"The list of hockey players who suited up in six different decades, including returning to the ice after being inducted into the Hall of Fame, is a short one: It starts and ends with Gordie Howe. But the list of kids who skated around the pond until dark, picturing themselves passing, scoring and enforcing like Howe, dreaming of hoisting the Stanley Cup like him — that one comprises too many to count. Howe's productivity, perseverance and humility personified his adopted hometown of Detroit, to which he brought four championships and which he represented as an All-Star more than 20 times. The greatest players define their game for a generation; over more than half a century on the ice, Mr. Hockey defined it for a lifetime. Michelle and I send our condolences to his sons and daughter, his family and his loyal fans from Hockeytown to Hartford to Houston and across North America."

JUSTIN TRUDEAU, CANADIAN PRIME MINSTER: "He was a gentleman, but he also was very much a tough guy. (He) showcased the best of what Canadians like to think of themselves as."

RYAN
GARZA/
DFP

CONTINUED FROM PAGE 67

teenage youngster. He enjoys swing music and malted milks. He is shy and afraid of the opposite sex."

YZERMAN AGAIN: "For all players fortunate enough to play for the Wings, we should take time to thank and honor Gordie, for he is a significant reason why Detroit is such a special place to play."

JOE SCHMIDT, HALL OF FAME LINEBACKER WITH THE DETROIT LIONS: "He was sort of a quiet guy when we'd get together. It was almost like he never wanted to talk about himself or say anything. You almost had to drag things from him in regards to his playing career and his playing ability. But I found him to be a fine gentleman and a great guy."

RICK SNYDER, MICHIGAN GOVERNOR: "His legacy in Michigan will carry on through the Gordie Howe International Bridge, which will stand as a united symbol between his home country and his adopted country, representing the teamwork he always embodied."

BILL FORD JR., EXECUTIVE CHAIRMAN OF FORD MOTOR CO. WHO ATTENDED GORDIE HOWE HOCKEYLAND SCHOOL IN ST. CLAIR SHORES: "He made a personal effort to know every player by name. Throughout life, when asked who my role models were, I always replied Henry Ford and Gordie Howe. I am grateful for his deep friendship over the years."

KEN HOLLAND, RED WINGS GENERAL MANAGER: "Gordie Howe was an incredible ambassador for the game of hockey.

The King and I

In 1954, Arnold Palmer won the U.S. Amateur at the Country Club of Detroit. Fifty years later, he hosted a charity tourney there featuring 24 past champs, such as Phil Mickelson and Lanny Wadkins. Gordie Howe surprised Arnie on the practice range at an event that raised $6 million for Cornerstone Schools.
KIRTHMON F. DOZIER/DETROIT FREE PRESS

He was as fierce and competitive as they come, but away from the rink he was truly engaging and personable and always enjoyed his interaction with fans. Gordie set the standard for this franchise during the Original Six era."

TED LINDSAY, HALL OF FAME LEFT WING AND LONGTIME TEAMMATE: "Gordie was larger than life, and he was someone who I thought would live forever."

RED BERENSON, COACH AND FORMER PLAYER FOR THE MICHIGAN WOLVERINES AND FORMER CENTER FOR

THE RED WINGS: "I followed his career because he was from Saskatchewan. When I got to Michigan, I couldn't wait to go see Detroit play and see Gordie Howe play. … My favorite number was No. 7, and my coach told me, 'No, no. You don't wear No. 7. You're in Michigan now. You wear No. 9.' Oh, yeah, No. 9. Gordie Howe. He said this is Gordie Howe country. I realized right away. When they gave me No. 9, I was pretty touched, even at the college level."

KIRK MALTBY, LONGTIME RED WINGS FORWARD: "You'd want to hear Gordie's hockey stories. You'd want to be within an ear's length so you could hear him, but at the same time, you didn't want to be right next to him because he'd get his fists and his elbows up. He'd get so animated. Thankfully there was never a hockey stick nearby."

NICKLAS LIDSTROM, HALL OF FAME DEFENSEMAN FOR THE RED WINGS: "His son Mark has told me stories of how tough he was as a player, but he was always a funny man when he came down to the locker room."

MIKE MODANO, HALL OF FAME CENTER WHO GREW UP IN WESTLAND, MICH.: "Great storyteller. Certain guys just go on and on, and Gordie was one of those guys. He just had a gift."

GARY BETTMAN, NHL COMMISSIONER: "Gordie's greatness travels far beyond mere statistics; it echoes in the words of veneration spoken by countless players who joined him in the Hockey Hall of

CONTINUED ON PAGE 69

"Let us pray he doesn't elbow too many angels."

CONTINUED FROM PAGE 68

Fame and considered him their hero. Gordie's toughness as a competitor on the ice was equaled only by his humor and humility away from it. No sport could have hoped for a greater, more-beloved ambassador."

WAYNE GRETZKY, HALL OF FAME CENTER: "Unfortunately we lost the greatest hockey player ever today, but more importantly the nicest man I have ever met."

PAVEL DATSYUK, LONGTIME RED WINGS CENTER: "World lost one of the greatest human beings and the best all-time hockey player. Thanks for many lessons and memories. RIP Gordie."

MARK KRAM, SPORTS ILLUSTRATED WRITER IN A 1964 PROFILE: "Despite an even temperament and a real distaste for combat, there is a part of Howe that is calculatingly and primitively savage. He is a punishing artist with a hockey stick, slashing, spearing, tripping and high-sticking his way to a comparative degree of solitude on the ice."

GRETZKY AGAIN: "To this day, my favorite Christmas ever was getting a Red Wings No. 9 jersey when I was five years old. It's still the best Christmas present I ever got."

Kids are all right

Among Colleen Howe's numerous charity endeavors, she relished her work with the March of Dimes. In 1972, the national poster girl, 8-year-old Carmen Donesa, wowed everyone, including Gordie, during her visit in the offices of Detroit Mayor Roman Gribbs.
JOHN COLLIER/DETROIT FREE PRESS

Mr. Tiger & Mr. Hockey

Tigers rightfielder Al Kaline and Red Wings right wing Gordie Howe, pausing under a shade tree at Plum Hollow in Southfield, Mich., were the biggest stars in the Motor City in the '50s and '60s — and darn good golfers for decades longer. **ALAN R. KAMUDA/ DETROIT FREE PRESS**

A Hall of Fame friendship

Sporting superstars bonded on the links, off the ice

GEORGE SIPPLE & MARK SNYDER

Throughout the 1950s and 1960s, the two iconic sports stars in Detroit were right wing Gordie Howe of the Red Wings and rightfielder Al Kaline of the Tigers. During their Hall of Fame careers, they became fast friends.

Howe joined the Wings as an 18-year-old in 1946. He retired at 43 in 1971. Kaline joined the Tigers as an 18-year-old in 1953. He retired at 39 in 1974.

Howe won his first scoring title with 86 points (43 goals, 43 assists) as a 22-year-old in 1951, 20 points ahead of runner-up Rocket Richard. Kaline won his American League batting title at .340 as a 20-year-old in 1955, 21 points ahead of runner-up Vic Power.

In an interview with the Detroit Free Press shortly before Howe suffered a serious stroke in October 2014, Kaline reflected on his relationship with Howe:

>> "Gordie's one of a kind. Of course, his nickname, Mr. Hockey, is exactly what he is. Other than the fact he was a great, great, great hockey player, he is one of the great people that I've ever run into in sports. Our friendship has gone back a long ways. We lived at one time close to each other."

>> "I used to go to hockey games with a friend of both of ours and afterwards we would go to Carl's steakhouse — which is no longer there — after the game before we went home. Several other players and their wives were always there, too. That's how I ran into Gordie."

>> "Gordie would come down to the ballpark once in a while and maybe take batting practice with us at that time in Briggs Stadium. When we started to go to dinner we got very friendly."

>> "He's such an icon in this city and in sports, especially in the hockey world."

Kaline, like an estimated 15,000 others, paid his respects to his old pal at a public visitation inside Joe Louis Arena four days after his passing at age 88. Mr. Tiger, now 81, told more stories about his time with Mr. Hockey — on the golf course, on the diamond, on the ice and in the public eye.

"I got to be very friendly with Gordie and played golf with him, mostly at Plum Hollow, and he was a very good golfer," Kaline said. "I just started playing, and he put up with me for a while." Kaline's game quickly improved, so much so that he later became a member at Oakland Hills Country Club, the most prestigious course in the state.

Kaline invited Howe to Briggs Stadium for a little BP.

"He had trouble hitting it for a while," Kaline said. "Then he hit one over the fence, and it was like he scored the winning goal in the playoffs."

Then Howe returned the favor at Olympia Stadium.

"I never skated before in my life," Kaline said. "I was a one-leg pusher on skates and holding on to the railing, and Gordie being Gordie came over and gave me one of his famous elbows. But he was a super person."

The Kalines and the Howes spent a lot of private time in each other's homes. When they were in public together, Kaline saw what he considered a real star.

"Certainly, Gordie was a much bigger name than me," Kaline said, "but people were always nice to us, maybe because of the personality. Gordie was so easy, so pleasant to be around. They showed respect, mostly for Gordie, which they should have."

Partners to the end

A lifelong love shined through for more than 55 years

SHAWN WINDSOR & GEORGE SIPPLE

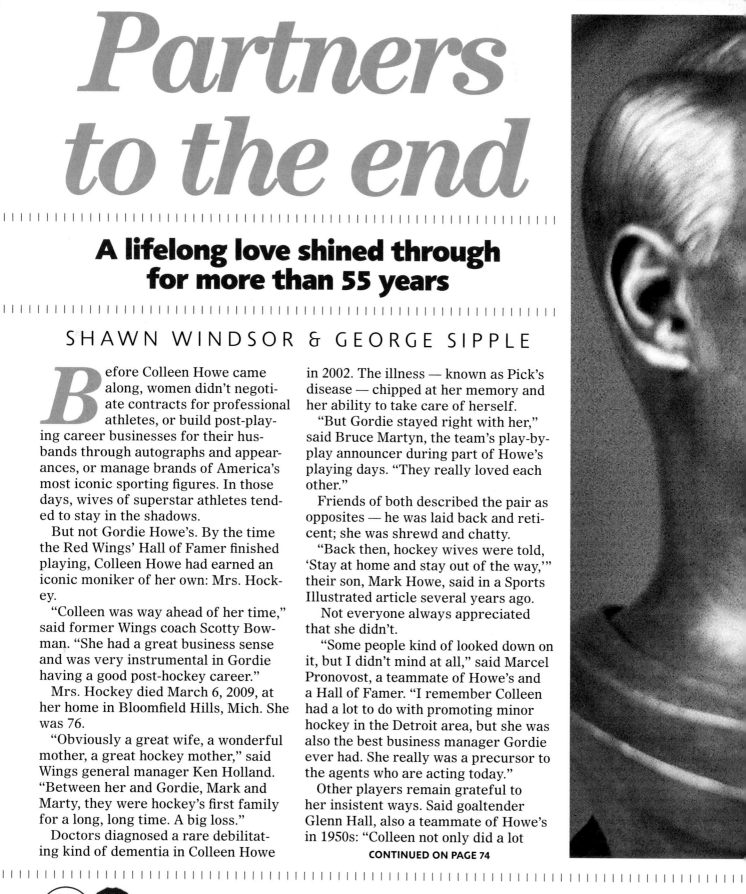

Before Colleen Howe came along, women didn't negotiate contracts for professional athletes, or build post-playing career businesses for their husbands through autographs and appearances, or manage brands of America's most iconic sporting figures. In those days, wives of superstar athletes tended to stay in the shadows.

But not Gordie Howe's. By the time the Red Wings' Hall of Famer finished playing, Colleen Howe had earned an iconic moniker of her own: Mrs. Hockey.

"Colleen was way ahead of her time," said former Wings coach Scotty Bowman. "She had a great business sense and was very instrumental in Gordie having a good post-hockey career."

Mrs. Hockey died March 6, 2009, at her home in Bloomfield Hills, Mich. She was 76.

"Obviously a great wife, a wonderful mother, a great hockey mother," said Wings general manager Ken Holland. "Between her and Gordie, Mark and Marty, they were hockey's first family for a long, long time. A big loss."

Doctors diagnosed a rare debilitating kind of dementia in Colleen Howe in 2002. The illness — known as Pick's disease — chipped at her memory and her ability to take care of herself.

"But Gordie stayed right with her," said Bruce Martyn, the team's play-by-play announcer during part of Howe's playing days. "They really loved each other."

Friends of both described the pair as opposites — he was laid back and reticent; she was shrewd and chatty.

"Back then, hockey wives were told, 'Stay at home and stay out of the way,'" their son, Mark Howe, said in a Sports Illustrated article several years ago.

Not everyone always appreciated that she didn't.

"Some people kind of looked down on it, but I didn't mind at all," said Marcel Pronovost, a teammate of Howe's and a Hall of Famer. "I remember Colleen had a lot to do with promoting minor hockey in the Detroit area, but she was also the best business manager Gordie ever had. She really was a precursor to the agents who are acting today."

Other players remain grateful to her insistent ways. Said goaltender Glenn Hall, also a teammate of Howe's in 1950s: "Colleen not only did a lot

CONTINUED ON PAGE 74

Apple of her eye

In "Gordie Howe's Son," Mark described how his parents turned into an item after one date in 1951: "The next day Dad left for Florida with some teammates, then home for the summer to Saskatoon, Saskatchewan, leaving the romance to bud by mail. My father was so worried about exposing his seventh-grade education, he wouldn't write a word without a dictionary by his side."

LIZ RAFFAELE/
DETROIT FREE PRESS

A sad day

Gordie Howe and son Mark leave St. Hugo of the Hills in Bloomfield Hills, Mich., after Colleen's funeral in 2009. Youngest son Murray said in a eulogy: "If you met Colleen Howe, you were immediately her friend. She would find out what you needed and then get it for you."
ERIC SEALS/DFP

CONTINUED FROM PAGE 72

for Gordie in promoting him after he retired, but the rest of the older players like myself got a spinoff benefit from it because instead of doing the card shows for nothing, we were finally getting paid for it. She did a bunch for all of us."

News of her death elicited reaction from Wings and beyond.

"Colleen was a pioneer hockey wife and hockey mom and devoted her entire life to the betterment of the game," said Wings owners Mike and Marian Ilitch in a statement. "She will be sincerely missed by us and all who knew her."

Added NHL commissioner Gary Bettman in a statement: She was a "formidable woman, the wife and partner of our iconic player, the matriarch of a remarkable hockey family."

Colleen Joffa was born in 1933 in Sandusky, Mich., where there's an ice arena bearing her name. She was living in Detroit when she met Gordie in April 1951 at the Lucky Strike Lanes on Grand River, near Olympia Stadium.

They married two years later.

In a 1999 interview, Gordie listed his formula for success: "Believe in youself. Love what you do. Follow your dreams. Overcome challenges. Believe in God. Marry the right girl." In another interview, Gordie revealed why he deferred to Colleen in business matters: "Girls have more time to think. They're not whacking each other over the head."

Colleen's contributions to hockey — beyond her husband's career — are numerous. She founded the first Junior A hockey team in the United States, the Detroit Junior Red Wings, trademarked "Mr. Hockey" and "Mrs. Hockey" and orchestrated the return of Gordie Howe to professional hockey when he played with sons Mark and Marty with the Houston Aeros of the upstart World Hockey Association in 1973.

She also developed the first private indoor ice hockey rink in Michigan, Gordie Howe Hockeyland in St. Clair Shores, and created the Howe Foundation in 1993.

CONTINUED ON PAGE 77

Mrs. Hockey Inc.

The Unknown Hockey Mom? Not quite. Among the dozens of business ventures Colleen Howe pursued in the '60s, '70s, '80s and '90s, she ran an extensive Amway distributorship while living in Connecticut. She kept an emergency supply of products in her Glastonbury garage.
HOWE FAMILY

Young love

Two years after Gordie Howe and Colleen Joffa met in 1951 at the Lucky Strike Lanes in Detroit, they were poolside on their honeymoon in Hollywood, Fla. They were married nearly 56 years when Colleen died in 2009. In "Gordie Howe's Son," Mark wrote: "Mom was far more taken by my father's sincerity than his celebrity. He blanketed her with a sense of security my mother had not known in childhood."

HOWE FAMILY

Up North

Colleen and Gordie Howe loved to spend warm summer days with their children at their cottage at Bear Lake in northern Michigan. In "Gordie Howe's Son," Mark wrote: "The one place where I always was a kid was at Bear Lake. ... The clear, spring-fed lake was stocked with rainbow trout and I would water-ski all day every day or go into the backwoods on a dirt bike." Gordie's mother, Kate, though, died falling down the stairs at the cottage.
HOWE FAMILY

CONTINUED FROM PAGE 74

Colleen Howe was the first woman inducted into the U.S. Hockey Hall of Fame. She also was honored as Michigan's Sportswoman of the Year in 1973.

In the fall of 1981, after her husband's career had ended with the Hartford Whalers, she was briefly a candidate for the Republican nomination for an open congressional seat in Connecticut.

And yet of all her accomplishments, perhaps none meant more to her husband than her daily, even hourly support of Mr. Hockey. He summed that up when he dedicated the Wings' 2007 book "Nine" honoring his career to her:

"I dedicate this book to my lovely bride Colleen. While I received the applause, you stood behind me and cheered the loudest. While I focused on improving my game, you made sure the bills were getting paid. While I was on the overnight trains and planes from city to city, you were tucking in the kids and teaching them to pray for their daddy. You have been my biggest fan. My agent. My dietician. My counselor. And even now as you battle for your life, you are my inspiration, my strength, and the love of my life."

Growing up with Gordie

A lack of money never meant a lack of values

MARK HOWE

It's a wonderful life
The Howe family loved water — whether in its frozen or liquid form. On a trip to Florida, Gordie took young sons Mark and Marty for a dip in the pool. Marty and Mark were born in Detroit 15 months apart — Marty in 1954, Mark in '55.
HOWE FAMILY

The ultimate uniform

Gordie Howe (Class of 1972) and Mark Howe (Class of 2011) owned matching jackets from the Hockey Hall of Fame in Toronto. They were the fourth father-son combo inducted.
HOWE FAMILY

In 2013, Hall of Fame defenseman Mark Howe wrote a warm, loving portrait of his life as a member of hockey's royal family, "Gordie Howe's Son: A Hall of Fame Life in the Shadow of Mr. Hockey." An excerpt:

Ifirst realized I had a famous father when he would take me places and everybody wanted his autograph. But I just thought that was normal. For as long as I remember, Gordie Howe had been my dad more than Mr. Hockey.

Interviewers have asked, "What's it like being Gordie Howe's son?" I've always assumed it was no different than being anybody's son who grew up in a loving, supportive family.

Of course, I felt differently the night he scored his 545th goal to pass Maurice Richard for the all-time lead in the NHL. I was eight years old and the cheering at Detroit's Olympia that night — Nov. 10, 1963 — seemed to last forever. I remember thinking, "Wow, I'm the only person in here who can say, 'That's my dad!'"

A wealth of pride, however, was the only wealth into which I was born. In

CONTINUED ON PAGE 80

A boy's life

As Gordie's son, Mark Howe enjoyed access to the Red Wings' dressing room. Dr. John (Jack) Finley, team physician from 1957-2003, visited with the pair of future Hall of Famers: Mark, then 5, and his father, 32. At least one of these three had been on the Wings' payroll since 1946.
FINLEY FAMILY

CONTINUED FROM PAGE 79

the '50s and '60s, not even being the planet's best hockey player translated into big dollars. When I came into the world on May 28, 1955 — 15 months after my brother Marty — Gordie Howe, the star of the Stanley Cup champion Red Wings, earned a salary of $10,000. That's worth $86,000 today, when the minimum NHL salary is $525,000.

Making the middle class was a huge step up for Dad, though. As the sixth of nine kids — another two were stillborn — of Katherine and Ab Howe, my father was raised in Saskatoon, Saskatchewan, in a house with no running water, necessitating that he shower at school. Thank God he liked oatmeal, which he sometimes had to eat three times a day. But the house in which his family lived so embarrassed him that until he made enough money to buy his parents a new place in Saskatoon, my father would not invite teammates to come visit over the summer.

Dad grew up delivering groceries in 30-below-zero weather and hunting the gophers that drove the prairie farmers crazy, which would bring in a dollar a tail. I'm told that because of his struggles in school, he was a really shy and under-confident guy away from the rink. But that was only part of the reason he eyed my mother, Colleen, for weeks at his Detroit hangout, the Lucky Strike Bowling Lanes near the Olympia, before finally approaching her. Dad didn't feel he had enough money for a proper date.

According to Mom, Dad was worried about making the mortgage payments when our growing family — Marty was five, I was four, sister Cathy an infant, and baby Murray on the way a year later — moved from the little ranch house on Stawell Avenue in northwest Detroit to the bigger, split-level home on Sunset Boulevard in Lathrup Village.

It seems amazing that the first time my grandparents ever saw their son play an NHL game was on Gordie Howe Night at the Olympia — in his

CONTINUED ON PAGE 81

Life-size celebration

The Red Wings weren't very good in 1966-67 — the last season for the Original Six. They finished fifth at 27-39-4, 14 points from the playoffs. Notable: The Wings set a record for fewest ties and Gordie Howe was "only" second-team All-NHL. At the eighth annual Face-Off Dinner at Cobo Hall, Howe received a six-foot cake to mark his 39th birthday the next day.
DETROIT FREE PRESS

Miracle on ice

Tired of driving her boys to Windsor, Ontario, to find indoor ice, Colleen Howe wondered why there weren't any indoor rinks around Detroit. She convinced a few friends in the early 1960s to build Gordie Howe Hockeyland, on Harper Avenue in suburban St. Clair Shores. To secure the loan, despite Gordie's concerns, they had to use their homes as collateral. "Not too bright," she wrote in "And … Howe!" "But we never gave it a second thought, because we were so convinced that this would really go and we really believed in it." Gordie wrote that Colleen should be in the Hall of Fame as a builder, for many reasons, including because Hockeyland "started the many thousands of other rinks to be developed, which opened up the facilities for American players." The Howes sold the building when they moved to Houston.
HOWE FAMILY

CONTINUED FROM PAGE 80

13th season. But you have to realize that there wasn't money to pay for their transportation to Detroit. Until we had the means to buy a second car, my mother would bundle Marty and me for trips to the train station as late as 4 a.m. in order to pick up Dad from road trips.

When he wasn't traveling, my father did what had been expected of him since he was a kid: helping cook and clean. Even after he could afford to do so, Dad wouldn't pay people to do work on the house that he could perform himself.

So Marty and I were given chores to earn our $5-a-week allowances. Even before I was old enough to be put in charge of cutting the lawn and removing snow, my once-a-week responsibility was to take everything out of our garage, clean it and then put everything back.

In our house, there were reprimands when we deserved them, but never any threats. Always, there was an awareness of our responsibilities, intensified by being Gordie Howe's kids.

Dad had struggled in school because he suffered from mild and undiagnosed dyslexia. When Detroit signed him at 16 out of a training camp in Windsor, Ontario — for a first-year pay of $2,300 and the promise of a Red Wings jacket — and sent him to a farm team in Galt, Ontario, he dutifully showed up for the first day of high school. But, suddenly realizing he knew no one, my father gave his books away, walked to a metal plant and took a job instead.

In his year at that factory, Dad actually worked his way into a low-level supervisory position. But he always regretted dropping out of school and felt that somebody from the hockey club should have stopped him. I think that's why he took up crossword puzzles — a big-time passion of his — to improve

CONTINUED ON PAGE 85

Year of the Beaver

In 1967, all the Howe children were in the same school — Lathrup Elementary School, which closed in the 1970s because of population shifts. From the left: Gordie, Mark, Cathy, Marty, Murray and Colleen, all in their Beavers sweatshirts.
HOWE FAMILY

Couples-only skate

Gordie Howe took a break from his duties with the Red Wings for a little recreational skating with Colleen soon after Gordie Howe Hockeyland opened in the 1960s. "When we'd go over to Hockeyland, Gordie would always want to go check back in the mechanical area to see how things were running," Colleen wrote in "And … Howe!"
DETROIT FREE PRESS

"The greatest thing my father passed on to me besides a sense of responsibility was a love of the game like his own."

MARK HOWE, on how he would race home to finish his homework so that he could go out to play hockey

Snow job

Of course, when Mark and Marty built a snowman outside the family home in Lathrup Village, they would use hockey sticks for arms. On the ice, Mark and Marty played on the same team until Mark was 12, when the midget-level Dearborn Fabricators decided Mark was too young and only a third-liner playing with boys 2-4 years older. Mark's bantam team, Myr Metal, won the national championship.
HOWE FAMILY

CONTINUED FROM PAGE 81

Now that's a fish

Forget the rainbow trout at Bear Lake! Mark Howe landed a 328-pound black marlin on a 1969 fishing excursion with Marty and Gordie in Ecuador. The boys were high school age; Gordie had turned 41. The family fished extensively their entire lives, and in the spring of 2015, after Gordie's stem-cell treatment, Mark and Murray took their father fishing for catfish on a Texas ranch, not far from sister Cathy's home in Lubbock.

HOWE FAMILY

his vocabulary. We did them together.

So it wasn't just Mom who valued education in the Howe household. Homework had to be done before I could get to my game, either at a rink or in my driveway. I would always race home from school to get it out of the way. Fortunately, school came pretty easily to me, because it was a means to an end. The greatest thing my father passed on to me besides a sense of responsibility was a love of the game like his own.

Dad also gifted me his ability to skate. Mom and Dad always said that while the other kids' ankles would bow in, mine would bow out for some reason — probably genetic. I'm told I learned at age 2 by leaning on a folding chair that I would push around the ice, giving me something to help pull myself up when I fell.

By age 4, I was playing on my first team: Teamsters 299, sponsored by the union. I remember a little about the outdoor rink — Butzel Arena — just up the street from our house in Lathrup Village. There were a couple of little bleachers and one tiny room where we could put our skates on. But you had to shovel the ice after it snowed.

Believe it or not, when I was really young, the Olympia was the only indoor rink in Detroit. My parents got together with some people and obtained the use of a closed factory in which they put up boards so that when it snowed you could still play, even if it was on natural ice in an unheated building. The train tracks that ran into the building were inactive, but as a five-year-old, I still worried about a train coming.

Mom and Dad created a rink in our front yard, too, setting their alarm clocks to come out at all hours of the night to move the hose they had attached to a ladder so they could flood the next section. Later, they put up wooden planks and plastic, which eliminated the need to move the hose. The lights I hung around the arena for

CONTINUED ON PAGE 87

Down the middle

In "Gordie Howe's Son," Mark told several golf tales: "Dad was a plus-handicap, and the day I shot par for the first time, at age 17, was also the first time I beat him. We were at Michaywe Pines near Gaylord, Mich. — the course had just opened — and we were tied going to the last hole. I birdied it while he bogeyed, and I won by two. That was VG-Day for me, boy, beating Gordie — not that I was competitive or anything. … For the Whalers' 1978-79 season, (Dad) was still defying time with almost a point a game until he took a shot off his foot. He kept playing on it until a second X-ray showed the fracture, and then, with the cast on, he shot a 75 on the golf course, claiming the plaster acted like an anchor and steadied him over the ball."

IRA ROSENBERG/ DETROIT FREE PRESS

CONTINUED FROM PAGE 85

play after dark also were used for our Christmas decorations, and one year we won an originality award from Lathrup Village.

Finally, a neighbor who owned a construction company came to our aid when he plowed a 200-by-85-foot rink — piled-up dirt served as the boards — in a vacant lot across the street. The town would open up a fire hydrant to flood the surface. That beat our little home rink in the front yard for reasons that included the location of the latter in front of a picture window, which I had broken one night when the puck bounced off the goalpost. Dad was away and it was cold. Mom was not a happy camper.

By my count, I broke 12 windows in the house over the years. When I was playing in the driveway, I usually had a net, but, always going for the corners, I would sometimes miss, so it was bang, bang, bang against the aluminum garage door. After hours of that one day, Mom finally came out and said, "Put the door up." So I did, and I think the very first ball I shot went through the garage, breaking the glass door leading into the kitchen and continuing down the hallway into the living room. In one straight shot, the ball ended up under the sofa at the far end of the house, leaving glass all over the kitchen.

Mom then asked me to put the door back down. She never told me to stop shooting, though. And we received encouragement from our parents about all of our passions, not just hockey.

Whatever pressure we felt came only from within. When Dad would attend our games, he would just watch, never yell or second-guess the coaching or do any of the things other parents would do. There wasn't a lot of unsolicited advice from him or from my mom. Basically, you learned how to do everything on your own, and when you had questions, they always were there with the answers. And I believe the sense of family that guided almost everything we did came not only from the big one in which Dad grew up, but from the one my mother never really had.

Her parents, Margaret Sidney and Howard Mulvaney — a trombonist who played with Benny Goodman, among other big bands — married and divorced young. Basically, Mom was raised by her great-aunt Elsie and great-uncle Hughie, who became the only people we knew well on that side of the family. The odd time at Christmas, we would go to Mom's mother's place in Detroit, but the relationship was not great.

Mom always tried to patch things up with her parents, make them at least OK, but deep down, they weren't. It's my belief she did so much work with children's charities because she drew a short straw when it came to her own parents.

Of course, she also couldn't do enough for her husband and children, which Dad never took for granted.

Because Dad was on the road or at practice or needing his nap on game days, Mom took charge of our hockey educations. She had some disagreements with the way minor programs were run by what was then the Amateur Hockey Association of the United States, so she formed some independent teams for us. Mom selected coaches not just to teach her boys, but everybody's on the club. After she had done her due diligence, I think she let the coaches, none of whom were screamers, do their thing.

Coping with greatness

Of course, the most essential hockey lesson Marty and I had to learn was how to cope with being the sons of the greatest player on earth. Even from a ridiculously early age, I would hear fans yelling, "You're not as good as your father," to which Marty sometimes would yell back, "Who is?" Pretty good answer. But as our teams, in search of better competition, would go to Canada to play games, there would be a lot more — and tougher — trash

CONTINUED ON PAGE 88

Off-season adventure

We're not in Lathrup Village anymore! Only 140 miles to Toronto. Or 280 back to Detroit. Where were the kilometers? Not in the 1960s. Gordie Howe and his oldest sons enjoyed Camp Weegeewa near Parry Sound, Ontario.
HOWE FAMILY

CONTINUED FROM PAGE 87

talk.

When our club became the first from the U.S. to enter the annual pee-wee tournament in Quebec City, there were around 14,000 people at Le Colisée. All eyes were upon Gordie Howe's eight- and nine-year-old sons, me on left wing, Marty on defense. Pretty intimidating. If, as we grew older, Marty ever fought any jealousy about me, the little brother becoming the better player in people's eyes, I don't think we ever discussed it. We spent most of our time talking about dealing with being Gordie Howe's kids. And the best advice on that came from our mom.

"You have to learn to let it go in one ear and out the other," she said. "It is what it is, learn to accept it. Maybe there's a negative side with all the attention you get. But let me make a list of all the positive things, like being able to go down to the Olympia and skate for six to eight hours. You can say, 'I'm Gordie Howe's son,' and go anyplace in that building you want."

Every Red Wing would get two tickets a game. Later in Dad's career, when Mom was too busy with running his business stuff to go to every game, I would go out onto Grand River, sell the tickets at the face value of $7.50 each, then walk past a friendly ticket taker and go sit in the press box.

A seat at the table

Fortunately, I never had to pay for a seat at our kitchen table with Bobby Baun, Bill Gadsby or other Red Wings after games, another perk of being Gordie's kid. Mom would let me stay up — I even got the meal ready for them

CONTINUED ON PAGE 89

Two down, two to come

In 1958, Colleen Howe posed with her bow-tie-clad boys in their Detroit home on Stawell Avenue. Cathy came on the scene in 1959 and Murray in 1960. With Cathy's arrival, the Howes decided they needed a bigger home and moved to suburban Lathrup Villiage.
HOWE FAMILY

Third generation

Gordie Howe showed his grandson Travis, Mark's first of three children, a trick or two about holding a hockey stick at a family Christmas in Connecticut. In Edmonton for a 1978 playoff game, Mark learned of Travis' birth while coming off the ice in pregame warm-ups. Travis Gordon Howe was the namesake of Lieutenant Colonel William Travis from the Alamo and You Know Who. Mark wrote in "Gordie Howe's Son:" "'Hey, Grandpa!' I said to Dad, congratulating him on his first, too, as I ran around the locker room with the news. I was on such a cloud nine. … I think I hit four posts, settling without the goal for my son that I had wanted in the worst way."
HOWE FAMILY

CONTINUED FROM PAGE 88

and drew the beers from the tap we had in the basement — and I would ask Frank Mahovlich about his aim on the goal he had scored that night, or question Baun about whether the shot he blocked had hurt him. Mostly, though, I just listened. My mother later said that at 9, I already was preparing myself to be a professional.

A couple of times a year, when Dad was supposed to be dropping Marty and me off at elementary school on the way to practice, I would plead to go to the rink with him, and every once in a while, he would say OK. Mom was fine with that because I was a conscientious student and she knew time with Dad was precious to us. When he was home during the day after practice, we would be at school. During the playoffs, the team would be in Toledo for up to four or five weeks because Jack Adams, the general manager, wanted the players away from "distractions" like wives

CONTINUED ON PAGE 90

Fourth generation

Little Ainsley receives the famous Gordie Howe elbow from her great-grandfather in June 2013. During his Hall of Fame induction speech in 2011, Mark Howe told his children, having watched his father's induction in 1972, that he knew how they felt and that they were the most important people in his life.
HOWE FAMILY

CONTINUED FROM PAGE 89

and kids. So when the Wings would be coming home late from a trip, I would ask Mom if I could wake up to see Dad for a little bit. She would say OK and I would get to spend 10 minutes with him before he would put me back to bed and get to sleep himself.

As long as my homework was done, I could go to the Wings games, even on school nights, which gave me the chance to see Dad some more. If the Wings were winning, I would leave my seat with about five minutes to go and stand along the barricade — the players had to go through the Olympia concourse to get to the locker room —

waiting for Dad to grab me and take me into the locker room.

Norm Ullman, No. 7 for Detroit, would always sit on one side of the bench. Dad, No. 9, was in the middle and Alex Delvecchio, No. 10, on the other side. I would sit with them while the coach would rant and rave. Dad remembered that once, when I was really young, I asked, "Who's that little fat guy?" meaning Jack Adams, and the next game, the policy was no more kids in the locker room. I don't know how long that rule lasted, but while Sid Abel, and then Gadsby, coached, it certainly no longer was enforced.

CONTINUED ON PAGE 92

GORDIE
90
9

Teammates forever

Only 15 months apart in age, Mark and Marty Howe were close on and off the ice. During his Hall of Fame speech, Mark said: "Marty, you are so much a part of this evening. We were teammates for 19 of my first 21 years of hockey. You looked out for me. You protected me. You're my big brother and my best friend." Marty played six seasons in the WHA (449 games, 67 goals, 117 assists, 184 points) and, most often on defense, parts of six more in the NHL (197 games, two goals, 29 assists, 31 points).

HOWE FAMILY

"You have to learn to let it go in one ear and out the other. It is what it is, learn to accept it."

COLLEEN HOWE, Mark and Marty's mother, on how to deal with the public pressure of being the oldest sons of Gordie in Detroit

Out for big ones

Gordie Howe, even in his 80s, never lost his love for fishing. In 2010, Mark took his father fishing at Peregrine Lodge in the Queen Charlotte Islands near Vancouver. The lodge's website boasted: "Home to the best salmon fishing in British Columbia and the Pacific North West."
HOWE FAMILY

CONTINUED FROM PAGE 90

Over to the left in the Wings' locker room was the stick rack. As I got older, I would grab a stick that Nick Libett or Dean Prentice would saw down to my size, and then the trainer, Lefty Wilson, would come out of the back, screaming at me (in mock anger) for stealing sticks. Everybody in the locker room would chuckle.

I wanted those sticks to play ball hockey on the stairs to the back balcony, where a railing and a wall created a sort-of goal. Even dressed up in my suit and tie — that's what you wore to the games in those days — I would go off to the balcony, hopefully with another player's kid — sometimes Jerry Sawchuk or Kenny Delvecchio — who could be the goaltender.

After Dad showered, he would sign every autograph, which I loved because that meant another 20 or 30 minutes to play on the stairs. But that also was

him again teaching me by example, showing how he took care of the public and what a humble man he was. Dad graciously accepted the many things offered his way, but didn't behave as though he had grown to expect them.

I saw him lose patience in public only three or four times. When, instead of asking nicely, somebody would demand an autograph with a "sign here!" Dad would usually sign the word "here." That's his sense of humor.

His thoughtfulness could be incredible.

Always, there had been this incredible grace to him.

A man of the people

One day, he playfully scooped up some ice shavings and threw them over the glass on some quadriplegic kids who were watching practice. One of them was laughing as the snow ran

CONTINUED ON PAGE 93

Youth movement

On this day in October 1966, Gordie Howe signed on for his 21st season — for $40,000-plus — and posed with 20-year-old rookies Peter Mahovlich (left) and Bart Crashley, who were born the same year he made his NHL debut and were jumping to the NHL without a stop in the minors, a team first since 1955. Howe, 38, said he hoped to play "as long as these hold out," pointing to his legs. He had been sidelined much of training camp with a knee sprain. Mahovlich played in the NHL until 1980-81, Crashley until 1975-76.

DICK TRIPP/DETROIT FREE PRESS

CONTINUED FROM PAGE 92

down his face, but when the next Red Wing did it, too, that kid was ticked off. He loved it only when Gordie Howe did it.

That's Dad's natural gift, a mystique or whatever you want to call it, the best part of what he was. His interaction with people was phenomenal.

In 1965, when I was 10, Dad signed a $10,000 yearly deal with Eaton's department store to travel coast to coast in Canada, visiting every store in the chain during July. Usually, when he got about halfway across the country, like to Winnipeg, I would fly out to travel with him for the final two weeks.

What I remember most about those trips were these picture cards he would pass out every day. Each night at 8 or 9, when we got back to the hotel, Dad would pre-sign 2,000 to 2,500 cards so that he could spend more time the next day writing in things like "To John, best wishes" and thus have a little more time for each person.

If it was a town with only one Eaton's, you would spend a couple of hours at the store, and then they would take us golfing or fishing. Marty, who wasn't a golfer but liked the fishing part of it, went a couple of times. Mostly, it was Dad and me. And every second with him was a treasure.

This excerpt from "Gordie Howe's Son" by Mark Howe with Jay Greenberg is printed with permission of Triumph Books. For more information, please visit www.triumphbooks.com/MarkHowe.

Red-hot smokin' Wings

For nearly 10 years, Detroit set the standard on the ice

NICHOLAS J. COTSONIKA

IN 1999, THE DETROIT FREE PRESS PUBLISHED "CENTURY OF CHAMPIONS: ONE HUNDRED YEARS OF MICHIGAN MEMORIES." AN EXCERPT FROM CHAPTER 4, TITLED "TWO DYNASTIES:"

When sports fans wanted to see the best of hockey and football in the 1950s, they turned their attention to Detroit. Nowhere else. With Gordie Howe smashing records and smashing opponents for the Red Wings, with Bobby Layne passing to teammates and passing out in bars for the Lions, no other city in North America came close.

Howe, a slope-shouldered forward from Canada, developed into the greatest all-around hockey player in history, and the Wings developed into the undisputed class of the NHL. From the 1948-49 season to 1954-55, the Wings continued their Ice Age by winning seven straight regular-season championships and four Stanley Cups — giving them seven Cups total, more than any other American franchise. Only their hated rivals, the Toronto Maple Leafs, had won as many.

Layne, a brash and boozing quarterback from Texas, led the Lions so well

CONTINUED ON PAGE 97

GORDIE 94 9

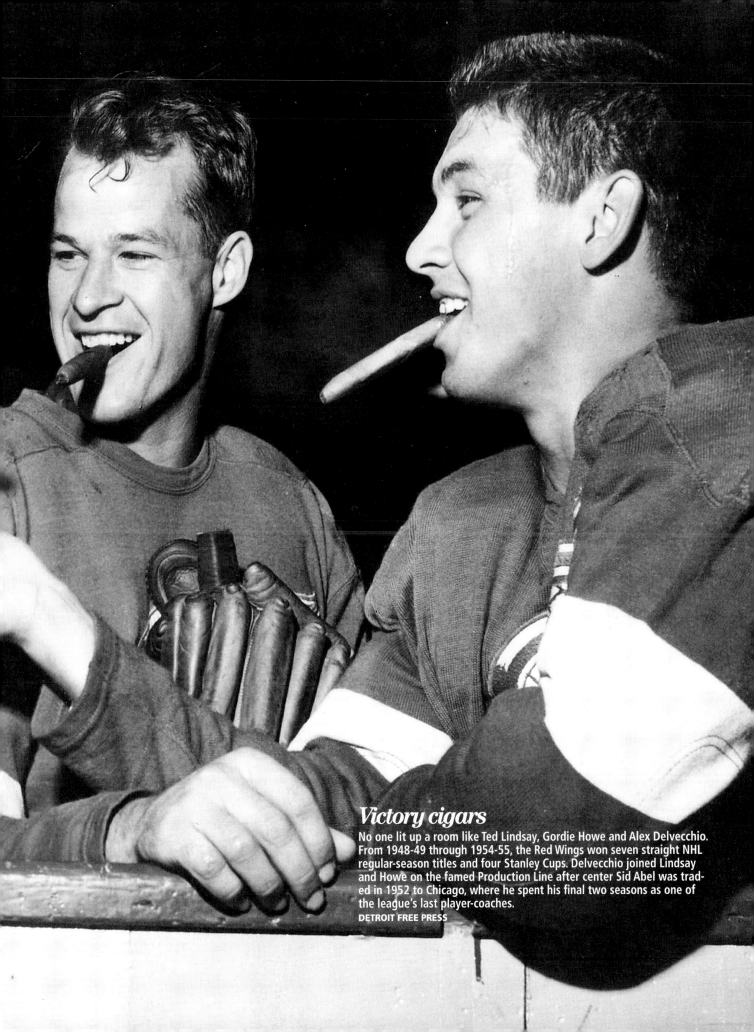

Victory cigars

No one lit up a room like Ted Lindsay, Gordie Howe and Alex Delvecchio. From 1948-49 through 1954-55, the Red Wings won seven straight NHL regular-season titles and four Stanley Cups. Delvecchio joined Lindsay and Howe on the famed Production Line after center Sid Abel was traded in 1952 to Chicago, where he spent his final two seasons as one of the league's last player-coaches.

DETROIT FREE PRESS

Record chase

On Oct. 13, 1963, Gordie Howe was an innocent by-stander when his 543rd career goal was disallowed. Referee Art Skov explained to captain Alex Delvecchio that he had whistled the play dead because Parker MacDonald was highsticking a Bruin. Howe, 35, was chasing Rocket Richard's record of 544 goals. He record-ed 543 for real in the third period, but 545 did not come for almost a month as Howe battled an ankle injury and the mob of reporters and photogra-phers chronicling his every move.

No. 545 came Nov. 10 at Olym-pia against the Canadiens, on a pass from Billy McNeill and on a shot an inch off the ice between Charlie Hodge and the right post. "Now I can start enjoying life again," Howe said. Montreal's Jean Beliveau visited Howe in the dressing room, delivering a painting of Mr. Hockey.

JIMMY TAFOYA/ DETROIT FREE PRESS

CONTINUED FROM PAGE 94

that they competed with the Cleveland Browns for the distinction as the NFL's dominant team. From 1951 to '57, the Lions won or shared four division titles and beat the Browns in three NFL championship games, winning five of the six playoff games in which they appeared. Fans packed Briggs Stadium to see them play, elevating professional football's popularity to that of the college game.

There were other teams to watch. The Tigers bid farewell to third baseman George Kell, who beat Boston's Ted Williams for the American League batting title in 1949, .3429 to .3427. They also introduced outfielder Al Kaline, who won the batting title in '55 with a .340 average — at age 20. The football programs at Michigan and Michigan State made news, and in '57, a pro basketball team nicknamed the Pistons arrived from Ft. Wayne, Ind., thanks to owner Fred Zollner.

Nevertheless, the Lions and Wings were kings. Life was good.

But if the story of Detroit in the fabulous '50s were a Shakespearean play, it would have been a tragicomedy. The people who built the city and its two dominant sports teams enjoyed postwar prosperity — in the factories, on the field and on the ice — but then made terrible mistakes, laying the groundwork for decades of hard times to come.

The auto industry kept humming, and the Motor City remained one of the nation's sparkling centers of manufacturing might. But as technology advanced, the industry decentralized, fought with labor unions and cut jobs. Affluent whites began branching out, riding away on the new superhighways in the cars they had built, slowly sprawling to the suburbs and deepening a racial divide that would explode in destructive violence.

The Wings and Lions kept winning, and the City of Champions label from the 1930s had not yet worn off. But as the teams' management meddled, their rosters disintegrated, stars went off to other teams, and those who were left behind became bitter. Losses started to pile up, and Detroit, which always held the highest standard of success, spent many of the coming years in want of winners.

And Howe!

In Detroit, the legend of humble Howe was known well by all: He never should have become known as Mr. Hockey with the Wings. He should have been a New Yorker. Should have died, too.

In 1942, at the age of 14, Howe attended a New York Rangers tryout in Winnipeg, Manitoba. He was homesick for Saskatoon, Saskatchewan, nine miles from the prairie town of Floral, his birthplace, and where he lived a life of deprivation and poverty as one of nine children. He didn't play well at all. In a few brief whirls on the ice, he did nothing exceptional, and the Rangers blew a golden opportunity. They sent him back to Saskatchewan. Unsigned.

A year later, Wings scout Fred Pinckney invited Howe to a tryout in Windsor, Ontario, and even bought him his first suit of clothes for the trip. Already 6-feet and nearly 200 pounds at age 15, Howe displayed his extraordinary skills. He was ambidextrous, and that caught the eye of coach and general manager Jack Adams. "Who's the big kid?" asked Adams, who didn't make the same mistake the Rangers did.

Impressed, Adams arranged for Howe to work out with a junior team in Galt, Ontario. As part of the deal, he promised him a Wings jacket. "I wanted that jacket so bad all the time I was in Galt," Howe said. "I remember that quite a few times I walked down to the railroad station by myself. I knew when the Red Wings' train would be coming through town, traveling to games. I'd just wait there for them. I figured that if they stopped for anything, I'd go aboard and see if I could ask Adams about my jacket. But the train never

CONTINUED ON PAGE 98

CONTINUED FROM PAGE 97

stopped. They went rolling through every time. I'd just walk back home."

In 1945, Howe was invited to training camp with the Wings, bunking in Olympia Stadium because of the wartime housing shortage. He amused himself by killing rats with his stick. After scoring two goals in an exhibition in Akron, Ohio, he signed his first contract to play for the Wings' farm club in Omaha, Neb. He scored 22 goals there. In '46, he made the big-league team for good — and approached Adams about some unfinished business.

"Mr. Adams," he said, "it has been two years now, and I haven't got my jacket yet." Adams sent Howe, along with forwards Ted Lindsay and Marty Pavelich, to a sporting goods store downtown and told him to sign for it. "It was smooth, like satin on the outside, with leather sleeves and an alpaca lining," Howe said. "It had a big 'D' with 'Red Wings' written on it. It looked like the most beautiful jacket in the world."

Had an incident in 1950 turned out for the worse, Howe wouldn't have been able to enjoy his prize jacket for very long.

In the playoff opener at Olympia, the Wings trailed Toronto in the second period, 3-0. Howe charged toward Leafs captain Ted (Teeder) Kennedy but, as he lunged to hit him, Kennedy pulled up. Howe missed him and went hurtling headfirst into the boards, right in front of the Detroit bench. Paramedics placed him on a stretcher as the crowd watched in stunned silence, then rushed him to Harper Hospital. He had broken his nose, shattered his cheekbone and seriously scratched his right eye and his brain was hemorrhaging from a fractured skull. He was in critical condition. His mother was flown in.

At 1 a.m., neurosurgeon Fredric Shreiber saved Howe and a hockey town's hopes. He drilled an opening in Howe's skull and drained fluid to relieve pressure on his brain. Afterward, he put

CONTINUED ON PAGE 101

Battle scar

Gordie Howe determined that he received some 400 stitches, mostly in his face, during his epic career. In January 1961, he had to deal with more than a 12-stitch wound. Toronto's Eddie Shack, about to be checked by Howe, struck him in forehead with the butt end of his stick. Howe suffered a concussion and spent a night in the hospital. Plus, he had to watch the Wings from the stands for bit.

DETROIT FREE PRESS

Nuptials on horizon

On April 2, 1953, the day after the Red Wings fell behind, three games to one, to the third-place Bruins, Gordie Howe and his teammates returned by plane from Boston, dropped by the Olympia for their mail and comp tickets, and headed by bus to Toledo, where they would stay before Game 5. The Free Press announced the day's big news in this headline: "Wedding Bells for Gordie." An interview with Colleen Joffa revealed the Calvary Presbyterian Church had been alerted for a ceremony about a week after the team's playoff run, "the Ted Lindsays would attend the couple," and only family and close friends would be invited. "I think he will make a wonderful husband," Joffa said. "I couldn't have picked anyone nicer and kinder than Gord." The Wings were ousted in six games, and the wedding occurred April 15 with Gordie's brother Vern as best man and Lindsay's wife, Joanne, as matron of honor. Marty Pavelich, Red Kelly and Lindsay were ushers.

DETROIT FREE PRESS

CONTINUED FROM PAGE 98

Howe in an oxygen tent. By morning, Howe's condition had improved. He pulled through, the only lingering effects of the operation being a facial tick, which earned him the nickname Blinky. As the story goes, while he lay on the hospital gurney he even apologized to coach Tommy Ivan, who had replaced Adams in 1947, for not playing better.

Howe went on to complete a spectacular 26-season NHL career in which he played 1,767 games, scored 801 goals, tallied 1,850 points, won six scoring titles, and took home six Hart trophies as the league's MVP. He played in 23 All-Star Games from 1948 to '80, when he skated at age 52 with the Hartford Whalers, still strong, playing with sons Marty and Mark.

No stupid boards would get the best of him. Nothing and nobody ever did. Howe was harder than them all.

Simply the best

In time, hockey would understand that Howe was above little things like head injuries. Like the Tigers' Ty Cobb, Howe was arguably the best ever to play his sport. Period. As great as Bobby Orr and Wayne Gretzky were, neither matched Howe's combination of scoring, toughness, intimidation and longevity. Howe was neither artist nor innovator. He played raw hockey, old-time hockey, Detroit hockey, ripping wrist shots and exploding elbows like atom bombs. To him, a hat trick wasn't three goals. It was a goal, an assist and a fight.

Howe never needed the help of enforcers. He was his own policeman, one of the best in the game. He once skated past a heckler in the crowd, and nicked the offender's nose with the blade of his stick, shutting him up. He often did

CONTINUED ON PAGE 102

He shoots …

Gordie Howe broke out as an elite scorer in the 1949-50 season. He scored 35 goals, runner-up to Rocket Richard's 43. His line finished 1-2-3 in the scoring race — Ted Lindsay with 78 points, Sid Abel with 69 and Howe with 68. Richard was fourth with 65.
DETROIT FREE PRESS

CONTINUED FROM PAGE 101

much more than nick opponents when they dared challenge him. In '59, Howe engaged in perhaps his most famous fight.

The Rangers that year promoted defenseman Lou Fontinato as the toughest player in hockey. New York-based Look magazine even presented a six-page picture spread on him, showing him flexing his muscles and looking mean. Whenever the Rangers played the Wings, Fontinato was on the ice with Howe. "The idea was to distract me," Howe said. After a few altercations one night at Madison Square Garden, Howe got even.

"Red Kelly and Eddie Shack were in a fight behind our net, and I'm leaning on the net watching it," Howe said. "Then I remembered a bit of advice from Lindsay: Always be aware of who's out on the ice with you. I took a peek and sure enough, there was Louie with his gloves off about 10 feet away and coming my way. I truly thought he was going to sucker-punch me. If he had, I'd have been over. I pretended I didn't see him, and when he swung, I just pulled my head aside and that honker of his was right there, and I drilled it. That first punch was what did it. It broke his nose a little bit."

A little bit? With one punch Howe made a mess of Fontinato's face and further solidified his reputation as the league's only one-man team. Even rival Maurice (Rocket) Richard, whom Howe felled with one punch in his first visit to the Montreal Forum in '46, eventually admitted Howe's overall superiority. "Sincerely, I have never seen a greater hockey player — I mean, a more complete player," Richard said. "Gordie Howe does everything and does it well." Chicago star Bobby Hull was just as blunt: "I wish I was half the player Gordie was."

Athletically, there was a little Howe couldn't do.

He was so strong from the waist up, he could outmuscle almost anyone.

CONTINUED ON PAGE 103

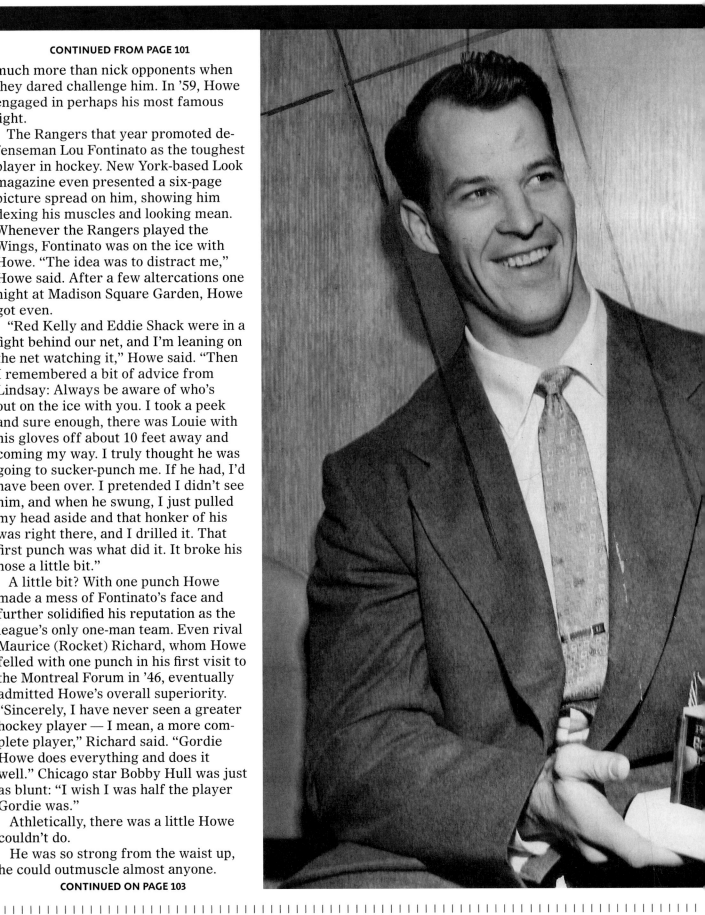

Award of the state

Despite a snowstorm in January 1954, fans packed the Sheraton-Cadillac Hotel for the Sports Guild awards, emceed by Budd Lynch. Gordie Howe received the hockey award. Other winners were the Tigers' Harvey Kuenn, the Lions' Bobby Layne, bowler Don Carter (from Pfeiffer Beer) and TV cowboy Justice Colt.
DETROIT FREE PRESS

CONTINUED FROM PAGE 102

In any sport. He was a wicked golfer, booming balls off the tee. He once played with 1954 PGA Championship winner Chick Harbert and outdrove him on every hole. Cleveland Indians manager Lou Boudreau invited Howe to take batting practice at Briggs Stadium. After seeing two pitches, Howe drove the third into the leftfield seats.

Howe spent some of his finest seasons playing with Lindsay and veteran captain Sid Abel as part of the Production Line, a scoring machine with a name that meshed well with Detroit's manufacturing image. The three were marvels to watch, taking long shifts of up to three minutes, crossing and crisscrossing in front of each other, banging the puck off a special spot on Olympia's boards to create scoring chances.

"Gordie would lead the charge down the right wing, and just after he crossed center ice, he'd fire the puck between the defensemen," center Murray Costello said. "If he hit the spot just right — and he was uncanny about hitting it — the puck came right out to the top of the left circle, and Lindsay would scoot in behind the defensemen and get a point-plank shot on goal."

The members of the Production Line were unselfish and unstoppable. In the 1949-50 season, Lindsay, Abel and Howe finished 1-2-3 in league scoring. "Those boys could score in their sleep," Adams said. All were stars, and Howe was just glad to be a part of the group, as he was just glad to wear that Wings jacket as a rookie.

Cup after Cup

Talent surrounded and supported Howe.

Lindsay was only 5-8, 163, but he was among the most aggressive players of

Annual ritual

Gordie Howe signed his contract with the Red Wings under the watchful eye of general manager Jack Adams. Although the undisputed best player in the sport, Howe was famously underpaid throughout his career. In "Gordie Howe's Son," Mark wrote: "Having married one of the most anxious-to-please men on earth — a multiple Hart Trophy winner who filled in a meager $1,000 raise on the blank contract that Adams put before him each year — my mother decided to protect her husband from himself, making sure he was properly compensated for the demands of his time."
DETROIT FREE PRESS

his time. He racked up 1,808 career penalty minutes and became known as Scarface, in tribute to the snaking stitches that held his features together. "I had the idea that I had to beat up everybody in the league," Lindsay said. "I'm still not convinced it wasn't a good idea." Lindsay was more than a brawler, of course. He could score. He could defend. He also took care of Howe, his best friend, who lived with him even after Lindsay got married.

Abel became Chicago's player-coach

CONTINUED ON PAGE 105

So good until so long

With Ted Lindsay on left wing and Gordie Howe on right wing, Detroit packed the NHL's best 1-2 scoring punch until the summer of 1957. At that point, Lindsay, 30, had been first-team All-NHL eight times and a member of four Stanley Cup champions. But he was dealt to Chicago, at least in part because of his union-organizing activities, which Howe didn't endorse in many players' view. For Lindsay and goalie Glenn Hall, the Wings received Johnny Wilson, Forbes Kennedy, Bill Preston and goalie Hank Bassen. Only Wilson managed even a 15-goal season, and Bassen posted a losing record over six seasons in the 1960s.

DETROIT FREE PRESS

CONTINUED FROM PAGE 103

Back in production

The original Production Line reunited in Joe Louis Arena in 1995 for the raising of Sid Abel's No. 12 to the rafters. Besides all their goals and awards, they were well-known for their incredible nicknames: Ted Lindsay — Terrible Ted; Abel — Old Bootnose; Gordie Howe — Mr. Hockey. Howe's No. 9 was retired in 1972, in a ceremony attended by Vice President Spiro Agnew, and Lindsay's No. 7 was retired in 1991.

MARY SCHROEDER/DETROIT FREE PRESS

in 1952, making way for Alex Delvecchio, who moved from left wing to play center on the Production Line. Fluid in his skating and precise in his passing, Delvecchio established himself as one of the best forwards ever to play in Detroit. He spent 24 seasons with the Wings, 11-plus as captain, and won the Lady Byng Trophy for sportsmanship and gentlemanly conduct three times.

Kelly and Marcel Pronovost were on defense. Kelly later helped build a dynasty as a center in Toronto, but as a Wing, he was the most dynamic defender in the game. He could rush the puck into the offensive zone like no one before Orr, yet rarely was beaten behind his own blue line. Pronovost played through pain as well as Howe, gutting through the '61 Cup finals with a broken ankle. At once a rugged player and a smooth skater, he continually put his body at risk for the team, as did Jack (Black Jack) Stewart.

Harry Lumley was steady in net early in Howe's career, winning the Cup in '50. But Adams traded him to Chicago to make room for Terry Sawchuk, who would become perhaps the best goaltender in history. Famously moody, Sawchuk battled opponents, referees and even fans on his way to four Vezina trophies and 103 shutouts, a league record. "Each day, I would say good morning to him in French and English," Pronovost said. "If he answered, I knew we would at least talk a little that day. But if he didn't, which was most days, we didn't speak the entire day."

There were others throughout the years who never received their due, such as center Norm Ullman, a ferocious forechecker who thrived in the playoffs but, because he wasn't flashy, found himself overshadowed. But no one disliked Howe and his bashful, goofy grin. No one was jealous. Howe never acted like a star. "We had great unity," center Glen Skov said. "We did a lot of things together off the ice. On the ice, we defied anybody to beat us."

CONTINUED ON PAGE 106

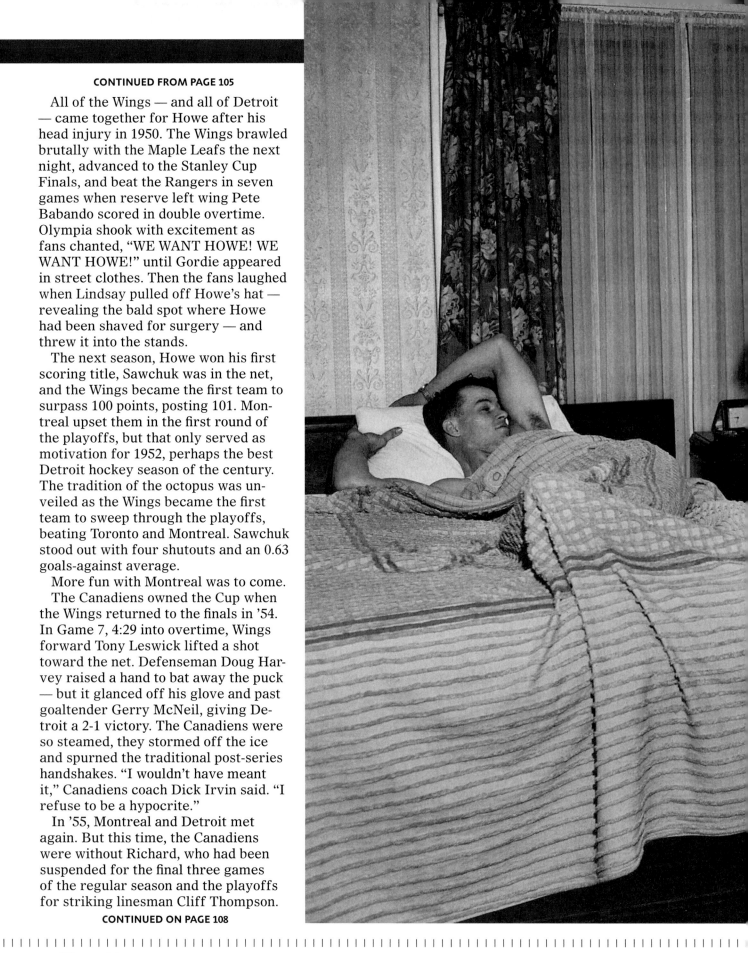

CONTINUED FROM PAGE 105

All of the Wings — and all of Detroit — came together for Howe after his head injury in 1950. The Wings brawled brutally with the Maple Leafs the next night, advanced to the Stanley Cup Finals, and beat the Rangers in seven games when reserve left wing Pete Babando scored in double overtime. Olympia shook with excitement as fans chanted, "WE WANT HOWE! WE WANT HOWE!" until Gordie appeared in street clothes. Then the fans laughed when Lindsay pulled off Howe's hat — revealing the bald spot where Howe had been shaved for surgery — and threw it into the stands.

The next season, Howe won his first scoring title, Sawchuk was in the net, and the Wings became the first team to surpass 100 points, posting 101. Montreal upset them in the first round of the playoffs, but that only served as motivation for 1952, perhaps the best Detroit hockey season of the century. The tradition of the octopus was unveiled as the Wings became the first team to sweep through the playoffs, beating Toronto and Montreal. Sawchuk stood out with four shutouts and an 0.63 goals-against average.

More fun with Montreal was to come.

The Canadiens owned the Cup when the Wings returned to the finals in '54. In Game 7, 4:29 into overtime, Wings forward Tony Leswick lifted a shot toward the net. Defenseman Doug Harvey raised a hand to bat away the puck — but it glanced off his glove and past goaltender Gerry McNeil, giving Detroit a 2-1 victory. The Canadiens were so steamed, they stormed off the ice and spurned the traditional post-series handshakes. "I wouldn't have meant it," Canadiens coach Dick Irvin said. "I refuse to be a hypocrite."

In '55, Montreal and Detroit met again. But this time, the Canadiens were without Richard, who had been suspended for the final three games of the regular season and the playoffs for striking linesman Cliff Thompson.

CONTINUED ON PAGE 108

Best of times

Gordie Howe and Ted Lindsay were more than linemates on the ice — they also roomed together at home and on the road. And, according to the photographer who snapped this picture, started their day with horseplay. Howe once wrote that Lindsay was "the most important presence in my life" before he married. They lived, like many Wings, in a Detroit boarding house run by a woman named Ma Shaw. It was not far from the Olympia and the Lucky Strike Lanes. Upon Howe's death, Lindsay, nearly 91, released a statement in which he reflected on a man he knew for 70 years, calling Howe "my longtime teammate and friend" and the "greatest hockey player who ever lived."
DETROIT FREE PRESS

CONTINUED FROM PAGE 106

Again the series went to seven games. Again, the Wings won. This time, Delvecchio was their hero, scoring two goals in the clincher and igniting a celebration some thought never would stop.

Writers became fond of comparing the Wings to the New York Yankees — an idea to which Adams responded by saying: "We are not the Yankees of hockey; the Yankees are the Red Wings of baseball." The Hockey News wrote that the Wings appeared primed to "imprison the Cup for all time." These were heady times. Montreal couldn't stop the Wings. Toronto couldn't stop the Wings.

In fact, only the Wings could stop the Wings.

Adams interrupted the '55 Cup victory party at the Book-Cadillac Hotel to give a speech on the intoxicating state of the team. He ticked off names. Howe. Lindsay. Delvecchio. Kelly. Then he told the crowd that some good young players were coming up. Ullman. John Bucyk. Larry Hillman. "If all of them come through," he said, "we'll be all right for the next few years."

The dynasty lasted but five more weeks.

Remembering the Wings' failures after previously winning a second straight Cup in 1937, Adams quickly broke up the team as he once promised he would, shipping out eight players and receiving no one of note in return. Skov, defenseman Benny Woit and left wings Leswick and Johnny Wilson went to Chicago for three lesser players. Sawchuk went to Boston in a nine-player deal to make room for up-and-coming Glenn Hall, then returned in '57 in a trade for Bucyk, who would become a Hall of Famer. "Jack Adams had this theory that if you were standing pat, you actually were losing ground," Howe said.

And so the greatest sports machine the Motor City had produced was dismantled, piece by piece, by the

CONTINUED ON PAGE 109

Can't keep a legend down

Gordie Howe, hurt and bleeding, struggled to get back on his feet in a January 1961 game against the Black Hawks. The Free Press wrote: "Goalie Glenn Hall pays no attention to his one-time teammate, but keeps his eyes on the action down the ice. It all turned out OK for the Wings, however. Howe was helped off for repairs, then returned to tee up one goal and score another in Detroit's 3-1 victory." A few months later, Chicago beat the Red Wings in six games to win the Stanley Cup, its first since 1938 and its last until 2010.

RAY GLONKA/DETROIT FREE PRESS

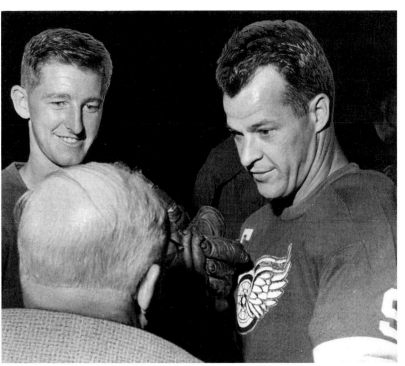

CONTINUED FROM PAGE 108

very man who built it. Some smelled the influence of the Norris family, grousing that the NHL actually stood for the Norris House League. James (Pops) Norris Sr. died in '52. Daughter Marguerite and son Bruce then ran the Wings; son James Jr. was chairman of the board of the Black Hawks; and the family owned a controlling interest in Madison Square Garden, which operated the Rangers. Trades to the Norrises' native Chicago seemed suspicious to agonized Detroiters.

In '57, Adams traded Lindsay — who had been making unwelcome noise about a union — to the Black Hawks with Hall as part of a six-player deal that brought back Wilson. Lindsay played with Chicago for three seasons, was retired in 1960-64, then came out of retirement in '64 to play one final season with the Red Wings. More puzzling moves led to more puzzling moves, leaving Howe, in the prime of his career, destined never to win another Cup. During one of his spurts as the Wings' coach, Abel told Howe to think positively. Howe replied: "Yeah, I'm positive Montreal has a damn fine team."

With Toe Blake as coach, Jacques Plante in goal and an array of sharpshooters up front, the despised Canadiens supplanted the Wings as the league's best. They won five consecutive Cups in 1956-60, then four out of five in 1965-69. The Wings returned to the finals in 1961, '63, '64 and '66 but didn't win another Cup until the New Ice Age, decades later, leaving the city forlorn. Adams was out in '62; he took over the Central Hockey League. He ended up a controversial figure, loved for his laughter and success, hated for his deviously demanding leadership style and miserable miscues.

"It was pathetic how Adams destroyed that team," Lindsay said. "Of course, there was an uproar about it. But Adams generally was respected for what he had done for the Wings in other years. And then he thought he was God anyway and could do no wrong."

The Lions' glory days ended much the same way.

The star of the All-Stars

Detroit's new hockey arena hosted a game full of future Hall of Famers — and none shined brighter than Gordie Howe

BILL DOW

Ageless wonder

A few weeks from his 52nd birthday, Gordie Howe lined up at right wing for the Prince of Wales Conference to start the NHL's 32nd All-Star Game. For Howe, it was his 23rd — and first in nine years. Of course, during those nine years he was busy retiring, unretiring and playing six seasons in the WHA. Howe recorded a third-period assist in a 6-3 Wales victory.

TONY SPINA/DETROIT FREE PRESS

*I*n 1980, Gordie Howe played in his 23rd and final NHL All-Star Game. At the time, he was a 51-year-old right wing with the Hartford Whalers. This midseason showcase would be a nod to the past — the legendary Howe was back in Detroit — and a glimpse to the future — a 19-year-old rookie sensation from a defunct league.

During his 26 NHL seasons, Howe missed an All-Star Game only once a decade (1947 — his rookie season — 1956 and 1966). His final one would be played at the NHL's newest venue — Joe Louis Arena along the Detroit riverfront, a few miles from Olympia Stadium, the "Old Red Barn" where Howe had toiled for 25 years.

Howe's final All-Star Game would include 14 future members of the Hockey Hall of Fame — and one already inducted member, Gordie. And it would include rookie Wayne Gretzky, who idolized Howe and would threaten in the decades to come to take his title as the greatest player ever.

Had the World Hockey Association not folded the previous year, hockey's two greatest icons would not have played against each other in a midseason showcase. After retiring from the Red Wings in 1971 — followed by two frustrating years as a club executive — Howe starred in the WHA for six years with Houston and New England, playing alongside sons Mark and Marty. Gretzky played for Indianapolis and Edmonton in the WHA in the 1978-79 season. After the league folded, Howe's Whalers and Gretzky's Oilers (along

CONTINUED ON PAGE 112

CONTINUED FROM PAGE 111

with Quebec and Winnipeg) merged into the NHL.

On Feb. 5, 1980, a crowd of 21,002 jammed into Joe Louis Arena to watch the Prince of Wales Conference play the Campbell Conference, setting an all-time attendance record — since broken — for a hockey game.

The game always will be remembered for the thunderous standing ovation fans showered upon Howe. For the pregame introduction, public address announcer John Bell wisely introduced Howe last, but not by name. It was hardly necessary.

"And from the Hartford Whalers, representing all of hockey, the greatest statesman for five decades, No. 9!" Bell announced as the fans quickly rose to their feet.

Witnesses said it felt like a 20-minute ovation, but in reality, the crowd stood and cheered for 2½ minutes, chanting, "Gor-die! Gor-die! Gor-die!" until Bell interrupted the roar by introducing national anthem singers Roger Doucet and Roger Whittaker.

On the CBC telecast, play-by-play announcer Dan Kelly remarked to color sidekick Dick Irvin: "Well, Mr. Irvin, I'd hate to see what happens if that No. 9 for the Wales Conference would score a goal. Do you think we'd finish the game?"

"I had the same feelings for the fans as they had towards me," Howe said in an interview 25 years later. "I was very emotional, and the fans were getting to me, so I skated over to Lefty Wilson on the bench and asked for help so I would be normal again. Lefty was bilingual — he spoke English and profanity. He said something to me I can't repeat, and it worked."

Wilson was the Wings' trainer.

But the man to whom Howe was eternally grateful was Scotty Bowman, who coached the Wales team against Al Arbour.

"When Scotty picked me to play, he really stuck his nose out because I

CONTINUED ON PAGE 114

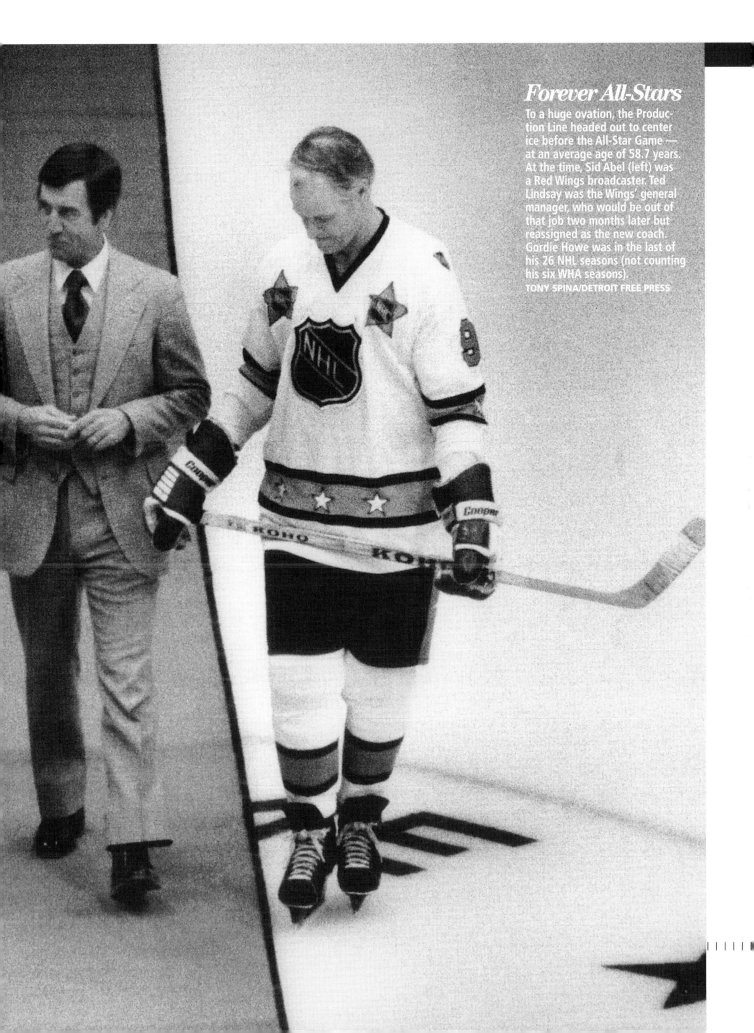

Forever All-Stars

To a huge ovation, the Production Line headed out to center ice before the All-Star Game — at an average age of 58.7 years. At the time, Sid Abel (left) was a Red Wings broadcaster. Ted Lindsay was the Wings' general manager, who would be out of that job two months later but reassigned as the new coach. Gordie Howe was in the last of his 26 NHL seasons (not counting his six WHA seasons).
TONY SPINA/DETROIT FREE PRESS

"I had the same feelings for the fans as they had towards me."

GORDIE HOWE, on how he reacted to a standing ovation from fans at Joe Louis Arena that lasted 2½ minutes

Thunderdome

Gordie Howe struggled to keep his composure during a thunderous ovation and chants of "Gor-die! Gor-die! Gor-die!" at the new Joe Louis Arena. His first shot, a snapper from between the face-off circles, hit Tony Esposito's left hand, forcing him out of the game. "I wish I'd had less time to think about it," Howe said. A quick wrister was kicked away by rookie sensation Pete Peeters. Another wrister went wide. Late, he was set up in the clear but Peeters made another stop. Howe did contribute an assist in the third period.
TONY SPINA/DETROIT FREE PRESS

CONTINUED FROM PAGE 112

later learned there was opposition to me playing," said Howe, who at the All-Star break had 11 goals. "I have so much respect for that man."

Bowman called Howe hockey's greatest player, and Bowman, coaching the Buffalo Sabres at the time, insisted that Howe play in the All-Star Game. Including the WHA, Howe played in 29 All-Star Games in five decades.

"I said if Gordie didn't play, I wouldn't coach," Bowman said. "It was a natural for him to play that game in Detroit. I didn't care what anybody thought. I knew he could still play, and it turned out perfect."

Every time Howe took a shift, the crowd cheered and chanted his name, hoping to see No. 9 turn the red light on again in Detroit. Near the end of the first period, Howe received the puck at point-blank range in front of Campbell Conference goalie Tony Esposito. Howe fired his famed snap shot at Esposito, who stopped the puck as the crowd groaned. The Black Hawks goalie promptly skated off the ice, having been injured by Howe's vicious shot.

"I wanted to shoot it low on his stick side, but I pulled it," Howe said. "I was unhappy with my performance because I missed that goal. I was nervous because I didn't want to make a fool of myself. Afterwards I wondered what the crowd would have done had I scored."

Howe's name was announced again on the loudspeaker, prompting a thunderous roar. Three minutes after Wings de-fenseman Reed Larson gave the Wales Conference a 5-3 lead, and with four minutes left in the game, Howe stole the puck twice before threading the needle on a perfect pass from behind the net. The puck went to Real Cloutier, who fired it past goalie Pete Peeters.

Gretzky didn't figure in the scoring for the Campbell Conference that night, but nearly all, including Howe, knew they were in the presence of a special player. Howe had first played against Gretzky the previous season in the WHA, and later that season he and Gretzky played on the same line with Mark Howe when the WHA All-Stars played the Moscow Dynamo.

Gretzky said that playing on a line with his boyhood idol was one of his greatest hockey thrills.

"You knew right away Wayne was going to be a great player," Howe said. "He was extremely smart and knew where everyone was on the ice. In the locker room I once parted his hair in the back to see if he had a third eye."

Gretzky peppered Howe with questions before they played the Russians, and Howe was happy to help out in the game.

"This one player kept slashing Wayne, so I told Wayne to flush him out on the left side and when he heard me coming get out of the way," Howe recalled. "He did it, and I walked right over the guy. When we got to the bench, they were fixing the guy up on the ice, and I said, 'Oh, God.' Wayne asked me what was wrong, and I said, 'He's getting up.' We had a great laugh."

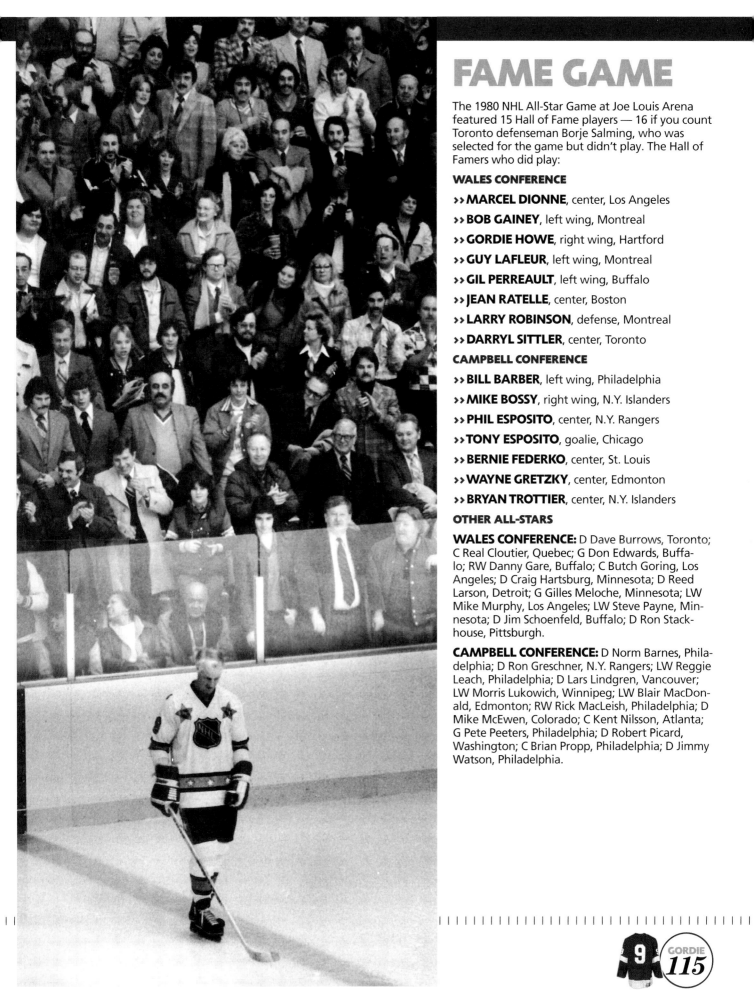

FAME GAME

The 1980 NHL All-Star Game at Joe Louis Arena featured 15 Hall of Fame players — 16 if you count Toronto defenseman Borje Salming, who was selected for the game but didn't play. The Hall of Famers who did play:

WALES CONFERENCE

>> **MARCEL DIONNE**, center, Los Angeles

>> **BOB GAINEY**, left wing, Montreal

>> **GORDIE HOWE**, right wing, Hartford

>> **GUY LAFLEUR**, left wing, Montreal

>> **GIL PERREAULT**, left wing, Buffalo

>> **JEAN RATELLE**, center, Boston

>> **LARRY ROBINSON**, defense, Montreal

>> **DARRYL SITTLER**, center, Toronto

CAMPBELL CONFERENCE

>> **BILL BARBER**, left wing, Philadelphia

>> **MIKE BOSSY**, right wing, N.Y. Islanders

>> **PHIL ESPOSITO**, center, N.Y. Rangers

>> **TONY ESPOSITO**, goalie, Chicago

>> **BERNIE FEDERKO**, center, St. Louis

>> **WAYNE GRETZKY**, center, Edmonton

>> **BRYAN TROTTIER**, center, N.Y. Islanders

OTHER ALL-STARS

WALES CONFERENCE: D Dave Burrows, Toronto; C Real Cloutier, Quebec; G Don Edwards, Buffalo; RW Danny Gare, Buffalo; C Butch Goring, Los Angeles; D Craig Hartsburg, Minnesota; D Reed Larson, Detroit; G Gilles Meloche, Minnesota; LW Mike Murphy, Los Angeles; LW Steve Payne, Minnesota; D Jim Schoenfeld, Buffalo; D Ron Stackhouse, Pittsburgh.

CAMPBELL CONFERENCE: D Norm Barnes, Philadelphia; D Ron Greschner, N.Y. Rangers; LW Reggie Leach, Philadelphia; D Lars Lindgren, Vancouver; LW Morris Lukowich, Winnipeg; LW Blair MacDonald, Edmonton; RW Rick MacLeish, Philadelphia; D Mike McEwen, Colorado; C Kent Nilsson, Atlanta; G Pete Peeters, Philadelphia; D Robert Picard, Washington; C Brian Propp, Philadelphia; D Jimmy Watson, Philadelphia.

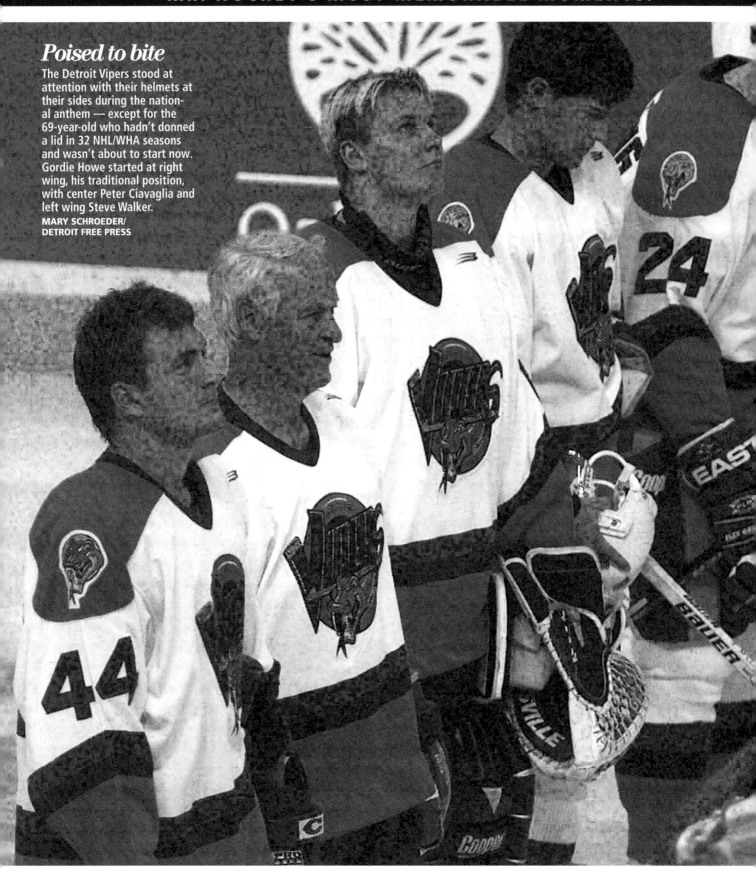

Poised to bite

The Detroit Vipers stood at attention with their helmets at their sides during the national anthem — except for the 69-year-old who hadn't donned a lid in 32 NHL/WHA seasons and wasn't about to start now. Gordie Howe started at right wing, his traditional position, with center Peter Ciavaglia and left wing Steve Walker.

MARY SCHROEDER/ DETROIT FREE PRESS

A new look for an old legend

A two-way player

On his lone shift, Gordie Howe tried the old bump 'n' run to slow down Iain Fraser, captain of the Kansas City Blades and 41 years his junior. Howe's previous game had been with the Hartford Whalers on April 11, 1980, a 4-3 overtime loss to Montreal that ended a three-game first-round sweep. Howe, who had a goal and an assist in the series, had only a two-minute penalty in his NHL swan song.

MARY SCHROEDER/DETROIT FREE PRESS

Even if it was just for 46 seconds, Gordie Howe made history at the Palace by playing in six decades of pro hockey

HELENE ST. JAMES

For 32 seasons — 26 in the NHL and six in the WHA — Gordie Howe reigned as the most feared man on the ice. Opponents shuddered at the thought of getting in the way of his renowned elbows.

But time shows mercy on no one, and it was a different Howe who skated through a 46-second shift in 1997 with the minor-league Detroit Vipers to become the first six-decade hockey pro.

His arthritis-hampered stride was much slower than in his heyday. He kept his elbows to himself.

And he actually was worried before he stepped on the ice at the Palace of Auburn Hills on Friday night Oct. 3.

"I just thought, 'Don't make a mistake,'" said Howe, 69 at the time and 17½ years removed from his last game with the Hartford Whalers.

Howe bumped Kansas City captain Iain Fraser during his shift, and watched a puck deflect off his leg and ricochet to Kansas City goalie Jon Casey.

"I almost got one," Howe said, laughing.

The Palace fans cheered his every move, even though his stick never touched the puck.

"That was beautiful," Howe said.

He called his bump on Fraser a smart defensive play.

"I know I don't have the speed," Howe said, "but when he took off, I thought, 'Oh, God.' It was just a casual

CONTINUED ON PAGE 118

The kings of longevity

During the first intermission, Gordie Howe chatted with Minnie Minoso, who also wore No. 9 and also played in six decades. Minoso, who started his baseball career in the Cuban and Negro leagues, played for the Indians in 1949, then for several teams in the '50s and '60s. At age 50 in 1976, as a publicity stunt directed by owner Bill Veeck, Minoso played three games and went 1-for-8 with the White Sox. He returned four years later with the Chisox and went 0-for-2. In 1993, at 67, he played in his sixth decade with the independent St. Paul Saints. In 2003, Minoso, who was a seven-time American League All-Star, played in his seventh decade, drawing a walk in another Saints game. He died in 2015 at 89.
MARY SCHROEDER/DETROIT FREE PRESS

CONTINUED FROM PAGE 117

bump of the lumber. It's pretty hard to forget old tricks."

Fraser called it differently: "I saw him stand in front of the net, and I wanted to — pow! — hit him. No, really, I didn't see him at first. I tried to get out of the way."

During his 25 seasons with the Detroit Red Wings, Howe won six Art Ross trophies as the NHL's top scorer and six Hart trophies as the league's MVP. Surely, it was amazing achievements like that that Wayne Gretzky was thinking of when his image appeared on the scoreboard to wish his boyhood idol luck. "You still are the greatest player that ever played," The Great One told Mr. Hockey.

After his history-making shift, Howe spent the rest of the first and all the second period on the Vipers' bench, watching the teams play to a 3-all tie. He wasn't on the bench for the final period, which ended 4-all. The Blades then won the shootout, 3-0, for a 5-4 opening-night victory.

During the first intermission, Howe and his wife, Colleen, came out to wave to fans, accompanied by son Marty and nine assorted grandchildren. Son Mark, a scout with the Red Wings, watched from the press box.

Howe first took to the ice a minute before 8 p.m., after a half-hour presentation commemorating the Vipers' first Turner Cup. While the championship banner was raised with the theme from "2001: A Space Odyssey" blaring in the background, Howe watched from the inflatable snake head that players had skated through since the Vipers' inaugural year four seasons earlier.

As the announcer began listing Howe's many accomplishments, the fans rose to their feet in anticipation of seeing Howe skate through the snake head and into the haze left by a five-minute pyrotechnics show.

Even his wife got a tear.

"As many times as I've seen Gord-

CONTINUED ON PAGE 120

Lace 'em up

To prepare for his pro return with the Detroit Vipers, Gordie Howe spent a little time skating with the team and talking with coach Steve Ludzik in his Palace office. Ludzik led the Vipers to the IHL's Turner Cup the previous season. After a practice, Howe said he was only two pounds over his old playing weight. "You only come around here once," he said. "I heard someone mention one time, life is our gift from God, what we do with it is our gift to Him. I'm still working on that. If I've got life enough left in me to do something that I think I can achieve, I'll go for it."
**MARY SCHROEDER/
DETROIT FREE PRESS**

ONE FOR THE AGED

Gordie Howe's one-shift comeback with the minor-league Detroit Vipers by the numbers:

0
Times Gordie touched the puck, or opponents touched Gordie.

1
Minutes it took the PA announcer to list Gordie's career feats.

2
Periods he sat on the bench, serenaded with occasional chants of "Gor-die! Gor-die!"

40.3
Average age of Gordie's line, with RW Gordie (69), C Peter Ciavaglia (28) and LW Steve Walker (24).

46
Seconds Gordie played in his record-setting shift.

3:41
Duration in minutes and seconds of standing ovation for Gordie.

7:59
Time of day Gordie skated out of the inflatable snake head.

OUCH!
Vipers defenseman Brad Shaw ripped a shot off Gordie's leg to goalie Jon Casey, who made the save.

CONTINUED FROM PAGE 118

ie play, I still got a lump in my throat when he came out," Colleen said. "I feel very blessed."

And the fans echoed her feeling. Every time his noble, white-haired mug appeared on the scoreboard, "Gor-die! Gor-die!" chants rang out. Even in the third period, after he had left the bench, fans called for him.

Besides his 25 seasons with the Wings, Howe spent four with the Houston Aeros, two with the New England Whalers and one with the Hartford Whalers. All told, he played in 1,767 NHL regular-seasons games and 419 more in the World Hockey Association. He also played in 235 pro playoff games — three full seasons worth of games.

His pro career started with 51 games for the Omaha Knights in the United States Hockey League in 1945-46 and ended with 46 seconds with the Detroit Vipers of the International Hockey League in 1997.

During those six decades, he left a lasting impression with millions of fans and his elbows with scores of players. His final shift came on an October night in Auburn Hills, Mich. His final center was Peter Ciavaglia, Harvard educated

A Great idea

Before his Vipers shift, Gordie Howe said that Wayne Gretzky, while chasing his scoring records in 1994, had suggested that Mr. Hockey "play a game with yours truly out in L.A. and get credit for six decades."
MARY SCHROEDER/DETROIT FREE PRESS

and 28 years old.

"The first shift of every new season is pretty exciting," said Ciavaglia, whose NHL career lasted five games. "But the thought of having Gordie Howe on the right wing is something else. It was a special moment.

"I won't have a shift like that again in my life."

Shield of Michigan is an independent lic

Gordie's final shift

After 46 seconds, Gordie Howe left the ice through the door on the Vipers bench. When it shut, the professional career of a legendary hockey player — one that went from Floral, Saskatchewan, to Auburn Hills, Mich. — finally came to an end. Howe was 69 years and 187 days young.

MARY SCHROEDER/ DETROIT FREE PRESS

Mr. 2,358

Breaking down Gordie Howe's points by the season

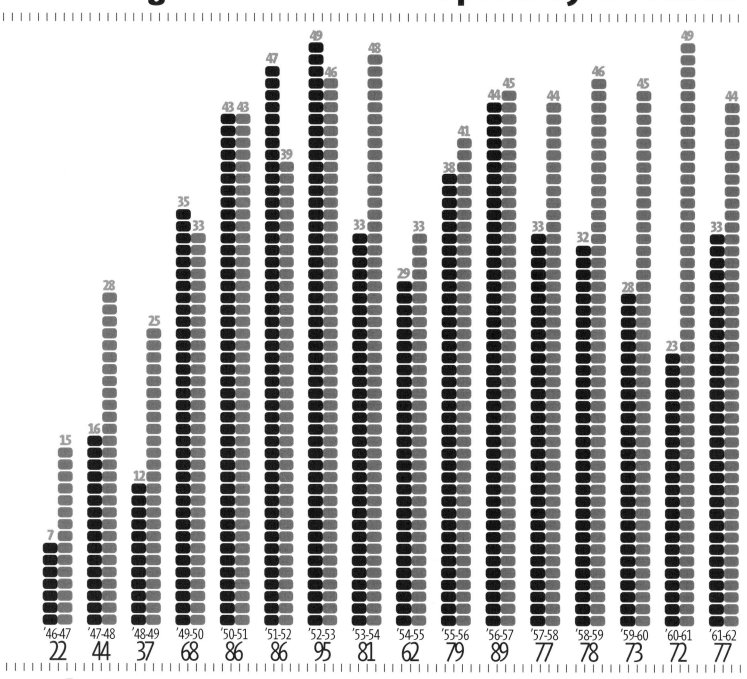

'46-47	'47-48	'48-49	'49-50	'50-51	'51-52	'52-53	'53-54	'54-55	'55-56	'56-57	'57-58	'58-59	'59-60	'60-61	'61-62
22	44	37	68	86	86	95	81	62	79	89	77	78	73	72	77

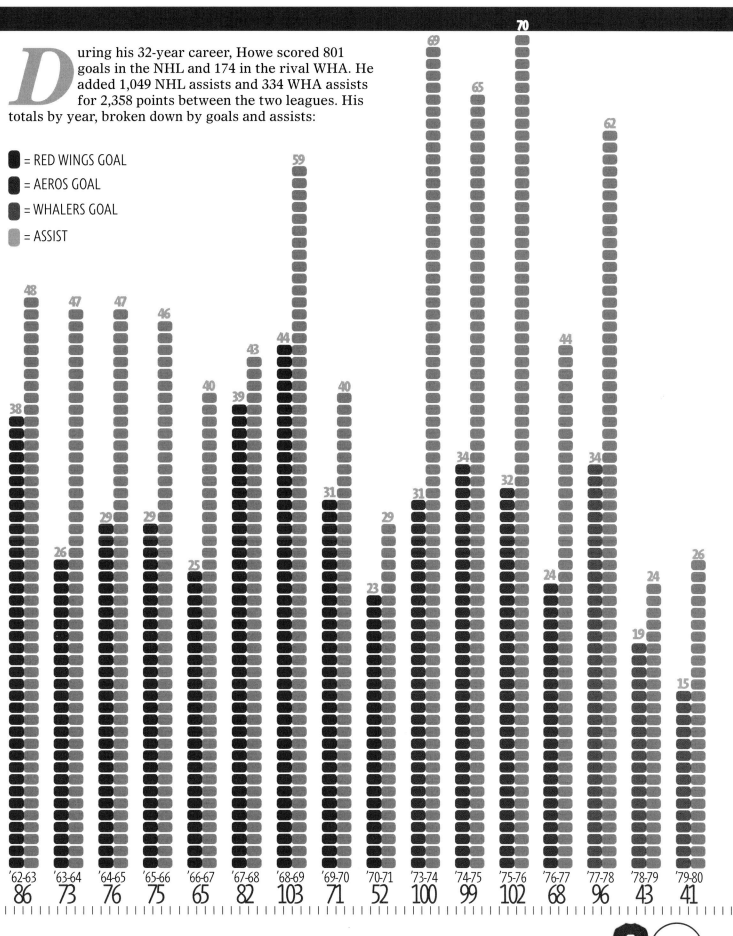

During his 32-year career, Howe scored 801 goals in the NHL and 174 in the rival WHA. He added 1,049 NHL assists and 334 WHA assists for 2,358 points between the two leagues. His totals by year, broken down by goals and assists:

= RED WINGS GOAL

= AEROS GOAL

= WHALERS GOAL

= ASSIST

Season	Total
'62-63	86
'63-64	73
'64-65	76
'65-66	75
'66-67	65
'67-68	82
'68-69	103
'69-70	71
'70-71	52
'73-74	100
'74-75	99
'75-76	102
'76-77	68
'77-78	96
'78-79	43
'79-80	41

REGULAR-SEASON STATISTICS

SEASON	AGE	TEAM	LG	GP	G	A	PTS	+/-	PIM	EV	PP	SH	GW	EV	PP	SH
							SCORING			GOALS				ASSISTS		
1946-47	18	Red Wings	NHL	58	7	15	22	—	52	—	—	—	—	—	—	—
1947-48	19	Red Wings	NHL	60	16	28	44	—	63	—	—	—	—	—	—	—
1948-49	20	Red Wings	NHL	40	12	25	37	—	57	—	—	—	—	—	—	—
1949-50	21	Red Wings	NHL	70	35	33	68	—	69	—	—	—	—	—	—	—
1950-51	22	Red Wings	NHL	70	43	43	86	—	74	—	—	—	—	—	—	—
1951-52	23	Red Wings	NHL	70	47	39	86	—	78	—	—	—	—	—	—	—
1952-53	24	Red Wings	NHL	70	49	46	95	—	57	—	—	—	—	—	—	—
1953-54	25	Red Wings	NHL	70	33	48	81	—	109	—	—	—	—	—	—	—
1954-55	26	Red Wings	NHL	64	29	33	62	—	68	—	—	—	—	—	—	—
1955-56	27	Red Wings	NHL	70	38	41	79	—	100	—	—	—	—	—	—	—
1956-57	28	Red Wings	NHL	70	44	45	89	—	72	—	—	—	—	—	—	—
1957-58	29	Red Wings	NHL	64	33	44	77	—	40	—	—	—	—	—	—	—
1958-59	30	Red Wings	NHL	70	32	46	78	—	57	—	—	—	—	—	—	—
1959-60	31	Red Wings	NHL	70	28	45	73	—	46	—	—	—	—	—	—	—
1960-61	32	Red Wings	NHL	64	23	49	72	—	30	—	—	—	—	—	—	—
1961-62	33	Red Wings	NHL	70	33	44	77	—	54	—	—	—	—	—	—	—
1962-63	34	Red Wings	NHL	70	38	48	86	—	100	—	—	—	—	—	—	—
1963-64	35	Red Wings	NHL	69	26	47	73	—	70	13	12	1	3	—	—	—
1964-65	36	Red Wings	NHL	70	29	47	76	—	104	13	12	4	2	—	—	—
1965-66	37	Red Wings	NHL	70	29	46	75	—	83	22	7	0	3	—	—	—
1966-67	38	Red Wings	NHL	69	25	40	65	—	53	16	8	1	1	—	—	—
1967-68	39	Red Wings	NHL	74	39	43	82	12	53	29	10	0	4	31	12	0
1968-69	40	Red Wings	NHL	76	44	59	103	45	58	35	9	0	6	42	17	0
1969-70	41	Red Wings	NHL	76	31	40	71	23	58	16	11	4	5	30	10	0
1970-71	42	Red Wings	NHL	63	23	29	52	-2	38	15	7	1	3	22	7	0
1973-74	45	Aeros	WHA	70	31	69	100	—	46	19	9	3	5	—	—	—
1974-75	46	Aeros	WHA	75	34	65	99	40	84	23	8	3	—	—	—	—
1975-76	47	Aeros	WHA	78	32	70	102	14	76	19	12	1	4	—	—	—
1976-77	48	Aeros	WHA	62	24	44	68	27	57	18	5	1	3	—	—	—
1977-78	49	Whalers	WHA	76	34	62	96	46	85	18	16	0	—	—	—	—
1978-79	50	Whalers	WHA	58	19	24	43	9	51	12	7	0	—	—	—	—
1979-80	51	Whalers	NHL	80	15	26	41	9	42	13	2	0	0	23	3	0
25 yrs		Red Wings	NHL	1,687	786	1,023	1,809	78	1,643	159	76	11	27	125	46	0
4 yrs		Aeros	WHA	285	121	248	369	81	263	79	34	8	12	—	—	—
2 yrs		Whalers	WHA	134	53	86	139	55	136	30	23	0	—	—	—	—
1 yr		Whalers	NHL	80	15	26	41	9	42	13	2	0	0	23	3	0
Career			NHL	1,767	801	1,049	1,850	87	1,685	172	78	11	27	148	49	0
Career			WHA	419	174	334	508	136	399	109	57	8	12	—	—	—

25, GOING ON 40

Howe is one of just five NHL players to score at least 25 goals in a season in which they were 40 or older. The list:

GORDIE HOWE 1968-69	JOHN BUCYK 1975-76	GORDIE HOWE 1969-70	TEEMU SELANNE 2010-11	JAROMIR JAGR 2015-16	DEAN PRENTICE 1972-73	TEEMU SELANNE 2011-12
44	36	31	31	27	26	26
AGE: 40.	AGE: 40.	AGE: 41.	AGE: 40.	AGE: 43.	AGE: 40.	AGE: 41.

PLAYOFF STATISTICS

					SCORING					GOALS			
SEASON	AGE	TEAM	LG	GP	G	A	PTS	+/-	PIM	EV	PP	SH	GW
1946-47	18	Red Wings	NHL	5	0	0	0	—	18	—	—	—	—
1947-48	19	Red Wings	NHL	10	1	1	2	—	11	—	—	—	—
1948-49	20	Red Wings	NHL	11	8	3	11	—	19	—	—	—	—
1949-50	21	Red Wings	NHL	1	0	0	0	—	7	—	—	—	—
1950-51	22	Red Wings	NHL	6	4	3	7	—	4	—	—	—	—
1951-52	23	Red Wings	NHL	8	2	5	7	—	2	—	—	—	—
1952-53	24	Red Wings	NHL	6	2	5	7	—	2	—	—	—	—
1953-54	25	Red Wings	NHL	12	4	5	9	—	31	—	—	—	—
1954-55	26	Red Wings	NHL	11	9	11	20	—	24	—	—	—	—
1955-56	27	Red Wings	NHL	10	3	9	12	—	8	—	—	—	—
1956-57	28	Red Wings	NHL	5	2	5	7	—	6	—	—	—	—
1957-58	29	Red Wings	NHL	4	1	1	2	—	0	—	—	—	—
1959-60	31	Red Wings	NHL	6	1	5	6	—	4	—	—	—	—
1960-61	32	Red Wings	NHL	11	4	11	15	—	10	—	—	—	—
1962-63	34	Red Wings	NHL	11	7	9	16	—	22	—	—	—	—
1963-64	35	Red Wings	NHL	14	9	10	19	—	16	—	—	—	—
1964-65	36	Red Wings	NHL	7	4	2	6	—	20	—	—	—	—
1965-66	37	Red Wings	NHL	12	4	6	10	—	12	—	—	—	—
1969-70	41	Red Wings	NHL	4	2	0	2	—	2	1	1	0	0
1973-74	45	Aeros	WHA	13	3	14	17	—	34	—	—	—	1
1974-75	46	Aeros	WHA	13	8	12	20	—	20	—	—	—	1
1975-76	47	Aeros	WHA	17	4	8	12	1	31	—	—	—	—
1976-77	48	Aeros	WHA	11	5	3	8	1	11	—	—	—	0
1977-78	49	Whalers	WHA	14	5	5	10	0	15	—	—	—	2
1978-79	50	Whalers	WHA	10	3	1	4	1	4	—	—	—	0
1979-80	51	Whalers	NHL	3	1	1	2	—	2	1	0	0	0
Career			NHL	157	68	92	160	—	220	2	1	0	0
Career			WHA	78	28	43	71	3	115	—	—	—	4

MR. HOCKEY'S TROPHY CASE

Gordie Howe's many awards in 32 seasons of NHL and WHA play:

HART TROPHY
Awarded to the NHL's most valuable player, as voted on by the media

'51-52 | '52-53 | '56-57 | '57-58 | '59-60 | '62-63

ART ROSS TROPHY
Awarded to the NHL scoring leader

'50-51 | '51-52 | '52-53 | '53-54 | '56-57 | '62-63

ALL-NHL FIRST TEAM
Voted on at the end of the season

'50-51 | '51-52 | '52-53 | '53-54 | '56-57 | '57-58

'59-60 | '62-63 | '65-66 | '67-68 | '68-69 | '69-70

ALL-WHA FIRST TEAM
Voted on at the end of the season

'73-74 | '74-75

DAVIDSON TROPHY
Award to the WHA's most valuable player

'73-74

ALL-NHL SECOND TEAM
Voted on at the end of the season

'48-49 | '49-50 | '55-56

'58-59 | '60-61 | '61-62

'63-64 | '64-65 | '66-67

STANLEY CUP

Given to the NHL champ each season

1950
1952
1954
1955—

AVCO CUP

Given to the WHA champ each season

1974 | 1975

LESTER PATRICK TROPHY

Presented by the NHL and USA Hockey for outstanding service to hockey in the United States

1967

NHL LIFETIME ACHIEVEMENT AWARD

Given to an NHL veteran in recognition of his overall contributions to the league and sport

2008

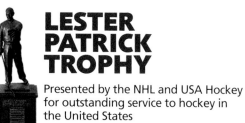

Tigers Drop Home Opener 5-3. Page 25

The Detroit Free Press

Whip Canadiens, 3-1, Keep Cup

RED WINGS WIN IT ALL

CIO, AFL May Unite in December

Delvecchio Gets 2 Goals in Finale

ON THE WING

Among the career franchise records Gordie Howe held with the Red Wings:

GAMES PLAYED
1,687

GOALS SCORED
786

POINTS SCORED
1,809

POWER-PLAY GOALS*
211

SEASONS LEADING TEAM IN POWER-PLAY GOALS*
13

HAT TRICKS*
18

GAME-WINNING GOALS*
121

SEASONS LEADING TEAM IN GAME-WINNING GOALS*
12

* As compiled by the Red Wings

9 GORDIE *127*

HOWE

9

1946-47   197

PORTRAIT OF "MR. HOCKEY" GORDIE HOWE BY ERIC MILLIKIN, BASED ON PHOTOS FROM SUSAN TUSA/DETROIT FREE PRESS AND DETROIT FREE PRESS FILES.